十二年國教特色招生及會考

全新英文閱讀專攻(上冊)目錄

Unit 1 ....P.1

Unit 2 ....P.3

Unit 3 ....P.5

Unit 4 ....P.7

Unit 5 ....P.9

Unit 6 ....P.11

Unit 7 ....P.13

Unit 8 ....P.15

Unit 9 ....P.17

Unit 10 ....P.19

Unit 11 ....P.21

Unit 12 ....P.24

Unit 13 ....P.26

Unit 14 ....P.28

Unit 15 ....P.30

Unit 16 ....P.32

Unit 17 ....P.34

Unit 18 ....P.36

Unit 19 ....P.38

Unit 20 ....P.40

Unit 21 ....P.42

Unit 22 ....P.44

Unit 23 ....P.46

Unit 24 ....P.48

Unit 25 ....P.50

Unit 26 ....P.52

Unit 27 ....P.54

Unit 28 ....P.56

Unit 29 ....P.58

Unit 30 ....P.60

Unit 31 ....P.62

Unit 31 ....P.64

Unit 33 ....P.66

Unit 34 ....P.68

Unit 35..P.70

Unit 36..P.72

Unit 37..P.74

Unit 38..P.76

Unit 39..P.79

Unit 40..P.81

Unit 41..P.83

Unit 42..P.85

Unit 43..P.87

Unit 44..P.89

Unit 45..P.91

Unit 46..P.93

Unit 47..P.95

Unit 48..P.97

Unit 49..P.99

Unit 50..P.101

Unit 51..P.103

Unit 52..P.105

Unit 53..P.107

Unit 54..P.109

Unit 55..P.111

Unit 56..P.114

Unit 57..P.116

Unit 58..P.118

Unit 59..P.120

Unit 60..P.122

Unit 61..P.124

Unit 62..P.126

Unit 63..P.128

Unit 64..P.130

Unit 65..P.132

Unit 66..P.134

Unit 67..P.137

Unit 68..P.139

Unit 69..P.142

Unit 70..P.144

Unit 71 ....P.146

Unit 72 ....P.148

Unit 73..P.151

Unit 74 ....P.153

Unit 75..P.155

Unit 76 ....P.157

Unit 77 ....P.159

Unit 78..P.161

Unit 79 ....P.163

Unit 80 ....P.165

Unit 1

題材　自然　　　　詞數　140　　　　建議閱讀時間　3.5分鐘

Years ago, many zoos kept all kinds of animals in small cages. Small cages made it easy for people to see the animals, but a small cage is not a good place for an animal to live in.

Today zoos keep animals in different kinds of cages. The cages are very big and open. They usually have plants and a little lake. The cages look like the animals' habitats.

Zoos help to protect all kinds of animals. They protect animals in the zoo and they protect animals in the wild. How do they do this? Zoos teach people how animals live in the wild. Zoos want people to help protect the animals' wild habitats.

Many plants and animals are going extinct. Mammoths, which are related with Asia elephants, are now extinct. Scientists say that seventy-four different kinds of living things go extinct every day!

Zoos are working together to stop animals from going extinct.

> cage：籠子　plant：植物　habitat：棲息地　protect：保護　wild：原野　extinct：絕種　Mammoth：長毛象　related：有關係的

閱讀上面的短文，選擇正確答案。

(　) 1. Zoos kept animals in small cages so that people can _____.
   A. protect them　　　　　　　B. see them better
   C. save them　　　　　　　　D. feed them

(　) 2. To protect animals, zoos _____.
   A. are trying to keep all kinds of animals
   B. are trying to free the animals
   C. teach people more about animals
   D. want people to feed the animals

(　) 3. A mammoth is a kind of _____ that has gone extinct.
   A. plant　　　　　B. bird　　　　　C. animal　　　　　D. tree

(　　) 4. An animal or a plant that is going extinct _____.

A. no longer exists in the world

B. comes into this world soon

C. becomes very dangerous

D. has fewer and fewer living members

【參考譯文】

多年前，許多動物園還把所有的動物都關在小籠子裏。小籠子便於人們看清這些動物，但不適合動物在裏面生活。

現在動物園把動物關在不同類型的籠子裏。這些籠子又大又開闊。裏面通常還有植物和小湖。這些籠子看上去有點像動物的自然家園了。

動物園有助於保護各種類型的動物。他們既保護生活在動物園裏的動物，也保護生活在野外的動物。他們怎樣做到這一點呢？動物園告訴人們動物在野外怎樣生活。動物園想讓人們幫助保護動物的自然家園。

許多動植物都將要滅絕了。比如長毛象，它是亞洲象的近親，現在就不存在了。科學家説，每天有 74 種不同種類的生物滅絕！

動物園正在共同努力以阻止動物的滅絕。

---

habitat　n.（動物的）棲息地，（植物的）生長地：This animal's natural habitat is the jungle. 這種動物的天然棲息地是叢林。

extinct　adj. 絕種的，已死的：Tigers are nearly extinct in the wild. 野生老虎快要絕種了。

mammoth　n. 長毛象（象的一種，已滅絕）

related　adj. 有聯繫的；有親屬關係的，屬於同一家族的：French and Spanish are related languages. 法語和西班牙語屬同一語系。

exist　v. 存在，生存，生活：Such a problem does not exist. 這樣的問題根本不存在。

【參考答案】

1. (B)　　　　　2. (C)　　　　　3. (C)　　　　　4. (D)

Unit 2

題材　廣告　　　　詞數　93　　　　建議閱讀時間　2.5 分鐘

Boston　Café

Monday~Saturday Lunch　　　**Sunday Evening**

12:00~14:00　　　　　　　　17:00~22:30

Lunch $6 (Under 10 $4)　　　Dinner $11 (Under 10 $6)

Monday~Thursday Evening

17:00~23:00　　　　　　　　Take Away

Dinner $11 (Under 10 $6)　　　$5 Each Box

Friday~Saturday Evening　　　(Put whatever you want into one box)

17:00~23:00　　　　　　　　Eat In

Dinner $12 (Under 10 $6)　　　All you can eat & Barbecue

Sunday Lunch　　　　　　　FREE Bottle of Wine

12:00~15:00　　　　　　　　for Each Table of Four

Lunch $7 (Under 10 $4)　　　(Evening and over 18 only)

Enjoy your meal!

Tel: 4655 9651

Green Avenue, Longridge

---

café：小餐館　take away：外帶　eat in：在餐廳內享用　meal：餐食
ad：廣告 (advertisement 的縮寫)

閱讀上面的短文，選擇正確答案。

(　　) 1. We can see this ad _____.
A. at a café　　B. at a library　C. at home　　D. at school

(　　) 2. We can go for lunch at _____ on Monday.
A. 10:30　　　B 12:30　　　　C. 11:45　　　D. 14:30

(　　) 3. Mrs. Peer will spend _____ if she goes for dinner on Friday.
A. $6　　　　B. $7　　　　C. $11　　　D. $12

(　　) 4. Mrs. Brown and his 8-year-old son had to pay _____ for dinner last Sunday.

        A. $7   B. $11   C. $12   D. $17

(　　) 5. You can _____ according to the ad.

        A. take away the food in one box for 8 dollars

        B. enjoy all you can eat and barbecue

        C. get a free bottle of wine with your friend

        D. call the Boston Cafe at 9651 7655

◀參考譯文▶

波士頓　餐　館

週一 ～ 週六　午餐	周日　晚餐
12點~14點	17點~22點30分
午餐 6美元 (10歲以下 4美元)	晚餐 11美元
	(10歲以下 6美元)
週一 ～ 週四　晚餐	
17點~23點	外帶
晚餐 11美元 (10歲以下 6美元)	每盒 5美元
	（想要什麼就裝什麼）
週五 ～ 週六　晚餐	
17點~23點	內用
晚餐 12美元 (10歲以下 6美元)	吃到飽和燒烤
周日　午餐	每桌 4人用餐時，
12點~15點	提供免費葡萄酒一瓶
午餐 7美元 (10歲以下 4美元)	（僅限晚餐，年齡18歲以上）

盡情享用吧！

電話：4655 9651

格林大街，朗裏奇

barbecue n. 燒烤：have a barbecue 舉行露天燒烤宴
avenue n. （城市中的）大路：Fifth Avenue （美國紐約的）第五大道

◀參考答案▶

1. (A)   2. (B)   3. (D)   4. (D)   5. (B)

Unit 3

題材　珍惜時間	詞數　132	建議閱讀時間　3.5 分鐘

Someone says, "Time is money." But I think time is even more important than money. Why? Because when money is spent, we can get it back. However, when time is lost, it'll never return. __1__ It goes without saying that time is usually limited. Even a second is very important. We should __2__ our time to do something useful.

But it is a pity that there are a lot of people who don't know the importance of time. They spend their limited time smoking, drinking and playing cards. They don't know that wasting time means wasting part of their own lives.

In a word, we should save time. __3__ Remember: we have no time to lose.

---
waste：浪費　It goes without saying：不用多說　limited：有限的　pity：可惜

閱讀上面的短文，選擇正確答案。

(　) 1.　A. That is why we waste time.
　　　　　B. That is why we mustn't waste time.
　　　　　C. That is why we have a lot of time.
　　　　　D. That is why we have no time.

(　) 2.　A. spend　　　　　　　　　B. waste a lot of
　　　　　C. keep　　　　　　　　　D. make full use of

(　) 3.　A. We had better leave today's work for tomorrow.
　　　　　B. We make today's work for tomorrow.
　　　　　C. We shouldn't leave today's work for tomorrow.
　　　　　D. We shouldn't use tomorrow's time.

【參考譯文】

　　有人說，「時間就是金錢。」但我認為時間甚至比金錢更重要。為什麼呢？因為錢花了可以再賺，而時間失去了卻永不回來。這就是我們不能浪費時間的原因。更不用說時間常常是有限的。即使一秒鐘也很重要。我們應該充分利用自己的時間去做些有用的事。

　　可惜的是，有許多人不懂得時間的重要性。他們把有限的時間花在抽煙、喝酒和玩牌上。他們不知道浪費時間就意味著浪費自己的生命。

　　總而言之，我們應該節約時間。我們不能把今天的工作留到明天去做。記住：我們的時間經不起浪費。

---

go without saying 不用說，理所當然（用 it 或 that 作主語）：It goes without saying that we shall all be glad when spring is here. 春天到來的時候，不用說我們都會很高興。/It goes without saying that the rich men have more power than poor men there. 不用說那裏的富人肯定比窮人更有權勢。

pity　n. 遺憾的事，可惜的事：It's a pity （that） you can't come to the party. 你不能來參加聚會真可惜。

【參考答案】

1. (B)　　　　2. (D)　　　　3. (C)

Unit 4

題材 知識普及　　詞數 196　　建議閱讀時間 5分鐘

Do you know something about tree rings? Do you know they can tell us what the weather was like, sometimes even hundreds of years ago?

A tree will grow well in a climate with lots of sunshine and rainfall. Little sunshine or rainfall will limit the growth of a tree. We can see the change of climate by studying the tree rings. For example, to find out the weather of ten years ago, count the rings of a tree from the outside to the inside. If the tenth ring is far from the eleventh ring, then we're sure that it was sunny and rainy most of that year. If it is near to the eleventh ring, then the climate was bad.

Tree rings are important not only for studying the history of weather but also for studying the history of man. Many centuries ago there lived a lot of people at a place in New Mexico. But now you can find only sand there—no trees and no people. What happened?

A scientist studied the rings of dead trees there. He found that the people had to leave because they had cut down all the trees to make fires and buildings. As all the trees had gone, the people there had to move.

climate：氣候　growth：成長　count：計算　weather：天氣　centuries：數百年

閱讀上面的短文，選擇正確答案。

(　　) 1.　＿＿＿＿ in good climate.
　　　　A. Tree rings grow far from each other
　　　　B. Tree rings become thinner
　　　　C. Trees will grow well
　　　　D. Trees don't need sunshine or rainfall

(　　) 2.　The scientists are interested in studying tree rings because tree rings can tell ＿＿＿＿.
　　　　A. whether a tree was strong or not
　　　　B. whether the climate was good or not
　　　　C. whether people took good care of the trees or not
　　　　D. how old the trees were

(　) 3. If you want to find out the weather of twenty years ago, you should study _____ of a tree from the outside to the inside.
   A. the twentieth ring
   B. the tenth ring
   C. the nineteenth ring
   D. the twenty-first ring

(　) 4. Why did people usually live in places with lots of trees?
   A. Trees could tell the change of the weather.
   B. Trees brought lots of sunshine and rain.
   C. Trees could make weather not too hot or too cold.
   D. Trees could be used for burning and building houses.

(　) 5. The people had to leave the place in New Mexico because _____.
   A. bad weather stopped the growth of trees
   B. they no longer had water and the land became sand
   C. they didn't have enough trees for burning
   D. there was too much rain there

◖參考譯文◗

　　你對樹的年輪瞭解嗎？你知道它們能告訴我們過去的氣候狀況、有時候甚至是幾百年前的氣候狀況嗎？

　　在陽光充足、雨量充沛的氣候條件下，樹會生長得很好。而缺少光照和降雨會限制樹的生長。通過研究年輪，我們能瞭解氣候的變遷。比如，要找出 10 年前的氣候狀況，從外到裏數一下樹的年輪就可以了。如果第 10 圈離第 11 圈較遠，我們就可以斷定，那年的大多數時候陽光和雨水都很充沛。如果離第 11 圈較近，那麼，當年的氣候就比較惡劣。

　　樹的年輪很重要，因為我們不僅可以用它們來研究氣候史，還可以研究人類史。許多世紀以前，在新墨西哥生活著很多人。但現在，那裏只能找到沙土——既沒有樹也沒有人。那裏到底發生了什麼？

　　一位科學家研究了那裏的死樹的年輪。他發現，人們必須離開，因為他們砍伐了所有的樹木用來生火和蓋房子。由於所有的樹木都不存在了，人們只得搬離。

> **ring** n. 圓圈，環形記號：They counted the rings of the tree after it was cut down. 這棵樹被砍倒後，他們數了數樹的年輪。
> **rainfall** n. 降雨量：This area has a very heavy rainfall. 這一地區降雨量很大。
> **limit** v. 限制：We must limit the expense to ￡10. 我們必須把費用控制在 10 英鎊。
> **growth** n. 生長，成長：A good diet is very important for children's growth. 良好的膳食對兒童的成長非常重要。

◖參考答案◗

　　1. (C)　　　　2. (B)　　　　3. (A)　　　　4. (C)　　　　5. (B)

Unit 5

題材 文化　　　詞數 181　　　建議閱讀時間 4.5分鐘

"Cool" is a word with many meanings. Its old meaning is used to express a temperature that is a little cold. As the world has changed, the word has had many different meanings.

"Cool" can be used to express feelings of interest in almost anything. When you see a famous car in the street, maybe you will say, "It's cool." You may think, "He's so cool." when you see your favorite football player.

We all maximize the meaning of "cool". You can use it instead of many words such as "new" or "surprising". Here's an interesting story we can use to show the way the word is used. A teacher asked her students to write about the waterfall they had visited. On one student's paper was just the one sentence, "It's so cool." Maybe he thought it was the best way to show what he saw and how he felt.

But the story also shows a scarcity of words. Without "cool", some people have no words to show the same meaning. Can you think of any other words that make your life as colorful as the word "cool"? I can. And I think they are also very cool.

---

meanings：意義　express：表達　temperature：溫度　famous：著名的
favorite：喜愛的　maximize：極大化　instead of：替代　scarcity：缺乏

閱讀上面的短文，選擇正確答案。

(　　) 1.　We know that the word "cool" has had _____.
A. many different meanings　　B. only one meaning
C. no meanings　　D. the same meaning

(　　) 2.　If you are _____ something, you may say, "It's cool."
A. afraid of　　B. interested in
C. unhappy with　　D. angry with

(　　) 3.　The sentence "It's so cool" on the student's paper may mean, "It looks really _____."
A. careful　　B. wonderful　　C. thankful　　D. painful

(　　) 4. The author takes an example to show that he feels_____ the way the word is used.

　　A. strange to　　　　　　　　B. pleased with

　　C. worried about　　　　　　D. excited at

【參考譯文】

「Cool」有許多意思，它最初表示溫度略微有點冷。隨著世界的變化，這個詞有了許多其他意思。

「Cool」可以用來表達使人感興趣的一切東西。當你看到街上有一輛名車時，也許你會說：「它真酷。」當你看到最喜歡的足球運動員時，也許你會想：「他真酷。」

我們都在擴大「Cool」的意思。你可以用它來代替許多詞彙，比如「新的」或「令人驚訝的」。爲了說明這個字的使用情況，這裏我們舉一個有趣的例子。一位老師要求學生寫一篇遊覽瀑布後的觀感，一位學生的紙上只有一句話：「它真酷。」也許他認爲這是表達所見所感的最好方法。

但這個故事也說明他詞彙的貧乏。沒有「Cool」，有些人找不到可以表達相同意思的詞。你能想出許多像「Cool」一樣令生活多姿多彩的其他詞嗎？我能，而且我認爲這些詞同樣很酷。

---

maximize v. 使增加到最大限度，最大化：We needed a new programme that would maximize the use of the country's existing airports. 我們需要一個新的計劃，以此來最大限度地利用國家現有的機場。

waterfall n. 瀑布：She watched the waterfall falling down the mountainside. 她看著瀑布從山坡上傾瀉而下。

scarcity n. 缺乏，不足，供不應求：There will be food scarcities in most regions. 大部分地區將會出現食物短缺。/The scarcity of building land has forced the price up. 建築用地不足迫使地價上升。

【參考答案】

　1. (A)　　　　2. (B)　　　　3. (B)　　　　4. (C)

Unit 6

題材　戰勝疾病　　　詞數　125　　　建議閱讀時間　3 分鐘

Recently, a successful war has been fought against one terrible disease: polio (脊髓灰質炎). Polio can make a person very sick. It can even kill. We have had polio vaccines for more than 40 years. But in many countries, people are poor, or they don't have enough information.

Some groups around the world have worked hard to give __1__ vaccines to children and adults. The United Nations has been a leader in the fight against polio. __2__ In 1988, there were 350,000 cases of the disease. In 2015, there were only 3,500. That is a drop of 99%.

Hopefully, the number will soon __3__. If we work together, we can win the war against polio and other diseases.

---
fought：(fight 的過去式和過去完成式)戰鬥　disease：疾病　vaccines：疫苗
information：資訊　adult：成人　drop：落下　zero：零　win：贏

閱讀上面的短文，選擇正確答案。

(　) 1.　A. many　　　　B. free　　　　C. few　　　　D. good

(　) 2.　A. They failed at last.
　　　　　B. They changed vaccines.
　　　　　C. They refused to accept the vaccines.
　　　　　D. They have had great success.

(　) 3.　A. rise up again　　　　　　B. go down to zero
　　　　　C. increase　　　　　　　　D. be under 10 percent

【參考譯文】

　　最近，針對一種可怕的疾病——脊髓灰質炎——的戰爭已經成功。脊髓灰質炎能帶來嚴重的後果，甚至能致人死亡。我們研製出脊髓灰質炎疫苗已經 40 多年了。但在許多國家，人們或者因為貧窮，或者因為缺乏足夠的瞭解而患上了這種疾病。

　　世界各地的許多組織經過艱苦努力已經能給兒童和成人發放免費的疫苗了。聯合國一直是針對脊髓灰質炎戰爭的領導者，他們取得了巨大的成就。1988 年，全世界有 35 萬人患有該種疾病。到了 2000 年，只有 3,500 人。患病人數下降了 99%。

　　我們希望這個數字能很快降到零。如果我們共同努力，我們就能贏得這場針對脊髓灰質炎和其他疾病的戰爭。

> **vaccine**　n. 疫苗：smallpox vaccine 天花疫苗
>
> **case**　n. 病例，病情：The doctors discussed her case fully. 醫生們全面地討論了她的病情。
>
> **hopefully**　adv. 如果希望實現，運氣好的話：Hopefully we will meet again on Thursday.
> 　　希望我們週四能再見面。

【參考答案】

1. (B)　　　　2. (D)　　　　3. (B)

Unit 7

題材　名人　　　詞數　159　　　建議閱讀時間　4 分鐘

O. Henry, a famous American writer of short stories, was born in North Carolina in 1862. O. Henry was a pen name. His real name was William Sydney Porter. When he was a young boy, he did not go to school for long because of being born in a poor family, but he tried to teach himself everything he needed to know.

When he was about 20 years old, O. Henry went to Texas. There he tried different jobs. He first worked on a newspaper, and then had a job in a bank. But he got himself into some trouble. Some money went missing from the bank. O. Henry was believed to have stolen it, so he was sent to prison. During the three years in prison, he learned to write short stories. After he got out of prison, he went to New York and went on writing.

He wrote mostly about New York and the life of the poor there. People liked his stories, because almost all of them finished with a sudden change. This made the readers surprised.

---
job：工作　trouble：麻煩　miss：不見了　stolen：(steal 的過去分詞)偷竊
prison：監獄　change：改變　sudden：突然的

閱讀上面的短文，選擇正確答案。

(　　) 1.　_____ was the real name of the famous American writer.
A. O. Henry　　　　　　　　B. William Sydney Porter
C. Texas　　　　　　　　　D. Carolina

(　　) 2.　O. Henry was sent to prison because _____.
A. people thought he had stolen money from the newspaper
B. he wanted to write stories about prisoners
C. people thought he had stolen money from the bank
D. he broke the law by not using his own name

(　　) 3.　Which of the following is true?
A. O. Henry was from a rich family.
B. O. Henry was in school for a long time.
C. O. Henry learned everything he needed by himself.
D. O. Henry liked writing stories when he was a little boy.

(　　) 4.　O. Henry got most information for his stories from _____.

A. his happy life as a boy

B. New York and the poor of the city

C. the newspaper

D. his life in prison

(　　) 5.　People enjoyed reading O. Henry's stories because _____.

A. they had surprising endings

B. they were easy to understand

C. they showed love for the poor

D. they were about New York City

【參考譯文】

　　歐·亨利是美國著名的短篇小說作家，他於 1862 年出生在北卡羅來納州。歐·亨利是他的筆名，他的真名叫威廉·西德尼·波特。在他還是個孩子時，由於家境貧寒，他很長時間沒有上學，但他努力自學必須掌握的所有東西。

　　到了 20 歲左右，歐·亨利來到德克薩斯。在那裏，他幹過各種工作。他先是在報社工作，後來又去了銀行。但他給自己找上了麻煩，銀行裏的錢丟了。有人認為是歐·亨利偷的，於是他被關進了監獄。在監獄的三年期間，他學會了寫短篇小說。出獄後，他來到紐約繼續從事寫作。

　　他寫的小說大多是關於紐約和那裏的窮人的生活。人們喜歡他的故事，因為這些故事的結尾幾乎都出現了突然的變化，這使得讀者們大為驚歎。

---

missing adj. 丟失的，下落不明的：She noticed one of the diamonds was missing. 她發現一顆鑽石不見了。

mostly adv. 幾乎全部地，主要地：She is mostly out on Sundays. 星期天她多半不在家。

prison n. 監獄：The thief was sent to prison for a year. 小偷被判一年監禁。

sudden adj. 突然的：The sudden arrival of guests forced her to change her plans. 客人的突然到來使她不得不改變計劃。

【參考答案】

1. (B)　　　2. (C)　　　3. (C)　　　4. (B)　　　5. (A)

Unit 8

題材　旅遊勝地　　　詞數　88　　　建議閱讀時間　2 分鐘

Sydney Tower

Address: 100 Market St, Sydney

Phone: 02 9333 9222

Fax: 02 9333 9203

Open time: 9:00 a.m. to 10:30 p.m. (Saturdays to 11:30 p.m.)

Ticket: $60 (for an adult) $30 (for a child)

Website: www.sydneytower.com.au

How to get there: train to Town Hall Station and a short walk along Market Street

How to book tickets: by phone/fax or through the web

Attraction: Sydney's best views are just the beginning! Sydney Tower takes you to the highest point above Sydney for exciting 360° views of our beautiful city.

閱讀上面的短文，選擇正確答案。

(　　) 1.　Sydney Tower is _____ in Sydney, Australia.
　　　　A. the busiest street　　　　　B. the biggest station
　　　　C. the highest point　　　　　D. the most beautiful park

(　　) 2.　If you want to book a ticket to Sydney Tower, you can't _____.
　　　　A. email sydneytower@hotmail.com
　　　　B. search www.sydneytower.com.au
　　　　C. fax 02 9333 9203
　　　　D. dial 02 9333 9222

(　　) 3.　Frank wants to go to Sydney Tower with his two children, he will pay _____.
　　　　A. $60　　　　B. $90　　　　C. $120　　　　D. $150

(　　) 4.　Last Saturday, Johnson went to visit Sydney Tower. He had to get down the tower _____.

A. after 11:30 p.m.　　　　　　　B. before 11:30 p.m.

C. at 10:30 p.m.　　　　　　　　D. by 10:30 p.m.

(　　) 5.　The passage above is probably _____.

A. a piece of news　　　　　　　　　　B. a conversation

C. a story　　　　　　　　　　　　D. an advertisement

【參考譯文】

雪梨塔

地址：雪梨市市場街 100 號

電話：02 9333 9222

傳真：02 9333 9203

開放時間：上午 9 點至晚上 10 點半 (週六至晚上 11 點半)

票價：60 美元（成人）30 美元（兒童）

網址：www.sydneytower.com.au

交通方式：乘火車至市政廳站，沿市場街步行一小段距離即到

訂票方式：電話、傳真或網絡

亮點：雪梨最美的風景就從這裏開始！雪梨塔帶你來到雪梨的最高點，讓你 360 度享受這座美麗城市令人興奮的景觀。

【參考答案】

1. (C)　　　　2. (A)　　　　3. (C)　　　　4. (B)　　　　5. (D)

Unit 9

題材　社會　　　詞數　137　　　建議閱讀時間　3.5分鐘

Although thousands of girls like him for his cute smile and strong body, Gary, 27, doesn't want to rest on his good looks. He made the move from modeling to acting six years ago, and now he is in a new field—singing. He works hard on his CDs.

Gary's life has had many ups and downs. After he dropped out of high school, he did many kinds of jobs before he became a model. Gary said that he got bad grades when he was in high school. But he was still very popular at school. "I was very active in the school and I liked to organize activities, so many teachers and students knew me." he said.

He hopes his teenage fans can learn from his life. "When you are in school, pay more attention to studies," Gary said. "Every young heart looks forward to entering the world outside. But _____. Finish your studies first."

閱讀上面的短文，選擇正確答案。

(　) 1. From the passage, we can know that Gary has done many jobs EXCEPT being _____.

　　A. a model　　B. a singer　　C. a teacher　　D. an actor

(　) 2. When he was in high school, Gary _____.

　　A. didn't like activities　　B. was very active

　　C. got good grades　　D. was not popular

(　) 3. Which of the following is the best to put in the "_____" in the last paragraph?

　　A. in no hurry　　B. bad luck　　C. not any more　　D. no idea

(　) 4. Gary tells his teenage fans _____.

　　A. to enter the outside world

　　B. to drop out of school

　　C. to study hard at their lessons

　　D. to take part in activities

---

cute：可愛的　modeling：模特兒界　acting：演藝界　field：行業

dropped out：輟學　organize：組織　attention：注意力　looks forward to：盼望

【參考譯文】

　　雖然有成千上萬的女孩因為他可愛的笑容和強健的體魄而喜歡他，但27歲的 Gary 並不想依靠自己的外表生活。六年前他從模特兒行業進軍演藝行業，而現在他又處於一個新的行業——歌唱。此刻他正專注於自己的唱片。

　　Gary 的生活有很多起起落落。在他輟學以後、成為模特兒之前，他做過各種各樣的工作。Gary 說，中學時自己的成績很差。但那時依然很受歡迎。「我非常活躍，喜歡組織各種各樣的活動，所以很多老師和學生都認識我。」他說。

　　他希望自己的粉絲能夠從他的生活中學到一些東西。「當你讀書時，一定要把更多的注意力放在學習上，」Gary 說。「每一個年輕的心靈都憧憬外面的世界。但是不能著急，一定要先完成學業。」

---

cute　adj. 可愛的，乖巧的：a cute child 逗人喜愛的小孩

drop out　退學，退出活動：Too many students drop out of college after only one year. 有太多大學生僅在學校待了一年就退學了。

up and down　（人生的）起伏："How are you managing?" "Oh, up and down, I suppose." 「你過得好嗎？」「哎，我想是時好時壞吧。」

【參考答案】

　　1. (C)　　　　2. (B)　　　　3. (A)　　　　4. (C)

Unit 10

題材　人與動物　　　　詞數　143　　　　建議閱讀時間　3.5 分鐘

For many years blind people used guide dogs to help them. Then someone had a good __1__. Why can't deaf people use hearing dogs?

Trainers agree that only some dogs can be trained as hearing dogs. The dogs must be __2__ and able to learn. The dogs must train for a long time. The deaf people must study, __3__. They learn how to work with the dogs.

Hearing dogs must listen for all kinds of __4__. Inside the home they listen for knocks __5__ the door, ringing telephones, and alarm clocks. __6__ listen for smoke alarms or strange sounds.

Hearing dogs also __7__ their owners outdoors. A deaf person __8__ hear if danger is near. A hearing dog will make the person __9__ if a car is coming. The dogs work hard all day long. For__10__ work, they will get hugs and treats.

閱讀上面的短文，選擇正確答案。

(　　) 1. 　A. rest 　　　　B. idea 　　　　C. night 　　　　D. time

(　　) 2. 　A. naughty 　　B. weak 　　　　C. foolish 　　　D. friendly

(　　) 3. 　A. neither 　　B. either 　　　C. too 　　　　　D. yet

(　　) 4. 　A. sounds 　　B. smells 　　　C. tastes 　　　　D. feelings

(　　) 5. 　A. for 　　　　B.by 　　　　　C. at 　　　　　　D. in

(　　) 6. 　A. She 　　　　B. They 　　　　C. It 　　　　　　D. You

(　　) 7. 　A. leave 　　　B. look 　　　　C. hurt 　　　　　D. help

(　　) 8. 　A. can 　　　　B. cannot 　　　C. needn't 　　　D. mustn't

(　　) 9. 　A. climb 　　　B. jump 　　　　C. stop 　　　　　D. lie

(　　) 10. A. good 　　　B. bad 　　　　　C. lazy 　　　　　D. careless

【參考譯文】

　　盲人使用導盲犬幫助他們已經有很多年了。後來，有人想了個好主意。聾人爲什麼不能使用助聽犬呢？

　　訓犬師認爲，只有經過訓練後的某些狗才能成爲助聽犬。這些狗必須對人友好，而且善於學習。這些狗還得經過長時間的訓練。聾人也必須學習。他們要學會怎樣和這些狗相處。

　　助聽犬必須學會分辨各種聲音。在室內，他們要學會分辨敲門、電話和鬧鐘的聲音。他們還得能聽出火警或是其他不尋常的聲音。

　　在室外，助聽犬也要幫助他們的主人。假如危險來臨，聾人是聽不見的。如果有車開過來了，助聽犬應該攔住自己的主人。這些狗整天都辛勤工作。如果表現出色，他們會得到擁抱和款待。

---

deaf adj. 聾的：She's been totally deaf since birth. 她生下來就是全聾的。
hug n. 擁抱：Give me a hug! 抱我一下！
treat n. 招待，款待：This meal is my treat. 這頓飯我請客。/Uncle took us to the circus as a treat. 叔叔請我們去看馬戲表演。

【參考答案】

1. (B)	2. (D)	3. (C)	4. (A)	5. (C)
6. (B)	7. (D)	8. (B)	9. (C)	10. (A)

Unit 11

題材 文娛與體育　　**詞數** 137　　**建議閱讀時間** 3.5 分鐘

Host: Hello! I'm Gavin from All Talk 970 FM. Welcome to our program. Today our topic is part-time jobs. Are they good for school children or not?

Headmaster: Certainly not. Children have got two full-time jobs already: growing up and going to school. Part-time jobs make them so tired that they fall asleep in class.

Mrs. Black: I agree. I know school hours are short, but there's homework too, and children need a lot of sleep.

Mr. Black: Young children perhaps stay at school until they're eighteen or nineteen. A part-time job can't harm them. In fact, it's good for them. They themselves earn their pocket-money. And they see something of the world outside school.

Businessman: You're quite right. Boys learn a lot from a part-time job. And we mustn't forget that some families need the extra money. If the students didn't take part-time jobs, they couldn't stay at school.

Host: Well, we have got two for, and two against. What do our listeners think?

---

host：主人，節目主持人　program：節目　topic：主題，話題　asleep：睡著
perhaps：或許　harm：傷害　pocket-money：零用錢　quite：十分　extra：額外的

閱讀上面的短文，選擇正確答案。

(　) 1.　How many guests join the discussion?
　　　　A. Three.　　　B. Four.　　　C. Six.　　　D. Five.

(　) 2.　Who have the same opinion?
　　　　A. Mr. and Mrs. Black.
　　　　B. The headmaster and the businessman.
　　　　C. The host and Mrs. Black.
　　　　D. The businessman and Mr. Black.

(　　) 3.　Mrs. Black thinks that children _____.

　　　　　A. need enough sleep

　　　　　B. need the extra money

　　　　　C. should see something of the world outside school

　　　　　D. should stay at school until they're eighteen or nineteen

(　　) 4.　What do the children think of part-time jobs?

　　　　　A. We are not told in this passage.

　　　　　B. Part-time jobs are good for them.

　　　　　C. Part-time jobs aren't good for their studies.

　　　　　D. Part-time jobs can help the students from poor families.

(　　) 5.　Where is the discussion most probably from?

　　　　　A. A TV station.　　　　　　　B. A radio station.

　　　　　C. A newspaper.　　　　　　　D. A magazine.

【參考譯文】

主持人：大家好！我是調頻 970《有話大家談》節目的蓋溫。歡迎來到我們的節目。今天我們的話題是兼職工作，你們認為兼職工作對學生有好處嗎？

校　長：肯定沒有好處。孩子們已經有兩項專職的任務了：成長和讀書。兼職工作會讓他們累得在課堂上睡著。

布萊克太太：我同意校長的說法。我知道在校時間是短的，但還有家庭作業，而且孩子們需要充足的睡眠。

布萊克先生：小孩子通常會在學校待到十八九歲。兼職工作不會傷害他們。實際上，兼職工作還對他們有好處呢。他們可以自己賺零花錢。還能看看學校外面的世界。

商　人：你說得很對。男孩子們能從兼職工作中學到很多東西。而且我們不要忘了，有些家庭需要額外的收入。如果孩子們不幹兼職工作，他們就無法待在學校。

主持人：好，現在有兩票贊成，兩票反對。聽眾朋友們怎麼想呢？

---

host　n. 主人，節目主持人：The event will be opened by television host Bill Punter. 這次活動將由電視節目主持人比爾·龐特揭幕。

topic　n. 主題，話題：His main topic of conversation is football. 他談話的主題是足球。

part-time　adj. 兼職的：I have a part-time job, about 20 hours a week. 我有一份兼職的工作，大約每週工作 20 小時。

for　prep. 贊成：Are you for or against the plan? 你贊成還是反對這個計劃？

against　prep. 不贊成，不支持，反對：She felt that everybody was against her. 她覺得每個人都在為難她。

【參考答案】

1. (B)　　　2. (D)　　　3. (A)　　　4. (A)　　　5. (B)

Unit 12

題材　個人情況　　詞數　172　　建議閱讀時間　4.5 分鐘

My name is Betty Sanders. I'm a telephone operator. My job is an interesting one. Today, for example, I had an interesting experience.

At 11 o'clock this morning, I got a call from a man. I don't know who he was. He was in trouble and worried about something. He gave me his address and asked me to send an ambulance right away. I asked him if somebody was hurt, but he didn't answer. He told me he needed a doctor at once, so I said I'd call an ambulance for him, but I still wanted to know what was wrong. Then he said, "Our keys are gone!" I didn't understand that! Why would he need an ambulance just because he couldn't find his keys? Then I found out what the trouble was.

The man and his wife left the car keys on a coffee table, and later they couldn't find them. Their little boy Johnny was playing in the room, and they thought he swallowed them.

But before I could help him, he told me he wouldn't need an ambulance any longer. His wife found the keys in her bag. They were there all the time.

> telephone operator：電話接線生　experience：經驗　worried about：擔憂
> ambulance：救護車　hurt：受傷　swallow：吞下去

閱讀上面的短文，選擇正確答案。

(　　) 1.　Betty Sanders works in a _____.
　　　　A. factory　　　B. shop　　　C. hospital　　　D. company

(　　) 2.　The man called Betty Sanders because _____.
　　　　A. he thought Betty was a doctor
　　　　B. he wanted to take an ambulance
　　　　C. he had lost his keys
　　　　D. his son was ill

(　　) 3.　In fact, his keys were _____.
　　　　A. swallowed by his little son　　　B. on a coffee table
　　　　C. left in the car　　　　　　　　D. in his wife's bag

(　　) 4.　From the passage we can see _____.
　　　　A. Betty Sanders likes her work
　　　　B. Betty's job is to answer long-distance calls
　　　　C. the man's little boy likes playing with keys
　　　　D. doctors can help people find keys

◀參考譯文▶

　　我叫貝蒂·桑德斯。我是一位電話接線生。我的工作很有趣。比如今天就發生了一樁趣事。

　　上午 11 點，我接到了一位男士打來的電話。我不知道他是誰。他有麻煩了，現在很著急。他告訴我他的地址，讓我立刻派一輛救護車過去。我問他，是否有人受傷了，他回答說不是，他說他急需一名醫生，於是我說我會立刻為他叫救護車的，但我還是想知道發生了什麼事。這時他說：「我們的鑰匙丟了！」我不明白這是什麼意思！他只是鑰匙找不見了，為什麼要叫救護車？後來我才知道是怎麼回事。

　　這位男士和他的妻子把車鑰匙放在了茶几上，但後來卻找不到了。他們的小兒子強尼正在這個房間玩耍，他們以為他把鑰匙吞下去了。

　　我還沒有能幫上他的忙，他就來電告訴我說，不需要救護車了。他的妻子在皮包找到了鑰匙。鑰匙一直就在那裏。

---

experience　n. 經歷，閱歷：That trip was an unforgettable experience. 那次旅行是一次難忘的經歷。

ambulance　n. 救護車：Don't worry—the ambulance is on its way. 別擔心——救護車在路上了。

swallow　v. 吞下：Liquid food may be more easily swallowed. 流質食物較易於吞咽。

◀參考答案▶

　　1. (C)　　　　2. (C)　　　　3. (D)　　　　4. (A)

Unit 13

| 題材 | 哲理 | 詞數 | 183 | 建議閱讀時間 | 4.5 分鐘 |

One day, a man came to Norman Vincent Peale, a famous writer. "Everything is gone, hopeless," the man said. "I'm living in the deepest darkness. In fact, I've lost heart for living."

Norman smiled and said, "Let's take a look at your situation." On a piece of paper, he drew a line down the middle. He suggested that they write on the left side the things the man had lost, and on the right, the things he had left. "You won't need the right side," said the man sadly. "I have nothing <u>left</u>."

Norman asked, "When did your wife leave you?"

"What do you mean? She hasn't left me. My wife loves me!"

"That's great!" said Norman excitedly. "Then that will be Number One on the right side—Wife hasn't left. Now, when were your children out of work?"

"That's silly. My children all have jobs!"

"Good! That's Number Two on the right side—Children have jobs," said Norman, writing it down.

After a few more questions in the same way, the man finally got the point and smiled. "Funny, how things change when you think of them that way," he said.

Change your thoughts and you change your world. If you paint a picture of bright future in your mind, you can put yourself into a happy situation.

---

situation：情勢，情況　suggest：建議　excitedly：興奮地　got the point：了解了
thoughts：想法　paint：畫　bright：光明的

閱讀上面的短文，選擇正確答案。

(　) 1. At the beginning, the man felt _____.
    A. silly   B. excited   C. hopeful   D. sad

(　) 2. What does the underlined word "left" in Paragraph 2 mean?
    A. 離開   B. 遺忘   C. 留下   D. 左邊

(　　) 3.　From the passage, we know _____.
　　　　　A. the man felt happy in the end
　　　　　B. the man's children all lost jobs
　　　　　C. the man's wife didn't love him
　　　　　D. Norman didn't help the man at all

(　　) 4.　Which is the best title for the passage?
　　　　　A. A story of a famous writer
　　　　　B. From the left to the right
　　　　　C. Living in the deepest darkness
　　　　　D. Change your thoughts, change your world

【參考譯文】

　　一天，一位男士來找著名作家諾曼‧文森特‧皮爾。「一切都完了，沒希望了，」他說，「我的生活一片漆黑。實際上，我已失去了活下去的勇氣。」

　　諾曼笑著說：「讓我們看看你現在的情形。」他在一張紙的中間畫了一條線，提議把那個男人失去的東西寫在左邊，把剩下的東西寫在右邊。「不需要右邊，」這個男人悲哀地說，「我一無所有。」

　　諾曼問：「你妻子何時離開你的？」

　　「你什麼意思？她沒有離開我，她很愛我。」

　　「太好了！」諾曼興奮地說，「這就是右邊的第一樣東西——妻子沒有離開。現在說說看，你的孩子什麼時候失業的？」

　　「真是愚蠢的問題，我的孩子都有工作。」

　　「那麼好，這是右邊的第二樣東西——孩子們都有工作。」諾曼邊說邊寫下來。

　　類似的幾個問題之後，這個人終於恍然大悟，他笑著說：「這可真有趣。當你用這種方法思考問題時，情況都變了。」

　　改變想法就能改變世界。如果你在腦子裏勾畫一幅光明的前途，你就能讓自己處於快樂的境地。

---

get the point　理解，懂得：I didn't get the point of his last remark. 我不懂他最後一句話的意思。

【參考答案】

1. (D)　　　　2. (C)　　　　3. (A)　　　　4. (D)

Unit 14

| 題材 | 乘坐電梯 | 詞數 | 180 | 建議閱讀時間 | 4.5 分鐘 |

　　Lifts are very useful. Why? Think about a __1__ building. You work __2__ the thirtieth floor. Maybe you can walk up all the stairs __3__. But can you climb thirty __4__ to your office every day? Of course not.

　　In an old lift, a worker is needed. He or she operates it __5__. In a modern lift, there is no worker. People can operate it __6__.

　　Do you know how to use a lift? OK, let me tell you. __7__, you want to go to the twelfth floor from the ground floor. First, you must press the button ▲, then the door opens. After that, you can __8__ the lift. Third, you press the ►◄, and the door closes. Fourth, you press the number 12, then the lift takes you up the twelfth floor. When the door opens again, you can get out of the lift. If you want to __9__ down to the first floor, you must press the ▼, then do the __10__. It will take you down there. It is very easy and fast. Now can you use it?

> lift：電梯　climb：登、爬　operate：操作　press：按、壓　button：按鈕

閱讀上面的短文，選擇正確答案。

(　) 1.　A. small 　　　　B. tall 　　　　C. long 　　　　D. nice

(　) 2.　A. for 　　　　　B.to 　　　　　C. of 　　　　　D. on

(　) 3.　A. one time 　　B. much time 　　C. all the time 　D.no time

(　) 4.　A. buildings 　　B. meters 　　　C. steps 　　　　D. floors

(　) 5.　A. in and out 　B. up and down C. on and off 　　D. here and there

(　) 6.　A. himself 　　　B. herself 　　　C. themselves 　D. ourselves

(　) 7.　A. In the end 　B. By the way 　C. For example D. As usual

(　) 8.　A. get into 　　　B. get up 　　　C. get out of 　D. get off

(　) 9.　A. run 　　　　　B. take 　　　　C. walk 　　　　D. go

(　) 10.　A. first 　　　　B. different 　　C. next 　　　　D. same

【參考譯文】

電梯很有用。爲什麼呢？想像一幢高層建築吧。（假如）你在第 30 層工作，也許你能走上去一次。但你能每天都爬 30 層到你的辦公室嗎？當然不行。

老式電梯需要有人在裏面操作。他（她）操縱它上上下下。新式電梯就不需要工作人員了，人們可以自己控制。

你知道怎樣使用電梯嗎？好吧，讓我告訴你。比如你想從第 1 層到第 12 層。你必須先按上升鍵，然後門開了。之後你進入電梯。第三步按關閉鍵，電梯門關了。第四步按數字 12，電梯把你帶到了第 12 層。當門再次打開時，你就可以出電梯了。假如你想去第 1 層，你必須先按下降鍵，然後做上述同樣的步驟。電梯將把你帶下去。電梯是非常快捷方便的。現在你會使用了吧。

【參考答案】

1. (B)	2. (D)	3. (A)	4. (D)	5. (B)
6. (C)	7. (C)	8. (A)	9. (D)	10. (D)

Unit 15

題材 學校生活　　詞數 153　　建議閱讀時間 4分鐘

On April 8, a report came out on the lives of high school students in China, Japan, South Korea and the US. About 6,200 students from the four countries were questioned.

Who studies hardest?

Nearly half of Chinese students spend more than two hours on their homework every day.

That's much more than students of the US(26.4%), Japan(8.2%) and South Korea(5.2%).

Who sleeps most often in class?

About 45% of Japanese students say they often sleep in class. In South Korea, it's 32%; in the US, 21%; and 5% in China.

Who is the most distracted?

American students are the most active in class, but 64.2% say they chat with friends in class; 46.9% say they eat food in class; and 38.9% say they send e-mails or do something else in class.

What do they do after school?

In their free time, most Chinese students study or surf the Internet. Most American students go out and play with their friends. Most Japanese students do sports. Most Korean students watch TV.

distracted：不專心的　chat：聊天　surf：瀏覽網頁

閱讀上面的短文，選擇正確答案。

(　　) 1. Who sleeps most often in class?
　　　A. Students from China.　　B. Students from the US.
　　　C. Students from Japan.　　D. Students from South Korea.

(　　) 2. 46.9% of the US students think _____.
　　　A. they sleep in class　　B. they eat food in class
　　　C. they go out and play
　　　D. they spend two hours on their homework

（　　）3.　What do Chinese students usually do in their free time?
　　　　　　A. They study or surf the Internet.
　　　　　　B. They watch TV.
　　　　　　C. They do sports.
　　　　　　D. They chat with friends.

（　　）4.　This passage probably comes from a(n) _____.
　　　　　　A. play　　　　　B. newspaper　C. story-book　　D. ad

【參考譯文】

　　4月8日，一篇關於中國、日本、韓國和美國中學生生活的報導見諸報端。大約有6,200名來自這四個國家的學生參與了調查。

誰學習最努力？

　　近一半的中國學生每天要花兩個多小時做家庭作業。

　　這個數字比美國學生（26.4%）、日本學生（8.2%）、韓國學生（5.2%）要高得多。

誰經常在課堂上睡覺？

　　大約45%的日本學生說他們經常在課堂上睡覺。在韓國，這個數字是32%，美國為21%，中國只有5%。

誰最容易分心？

　　美國學生在課堂上最活躍，但64.2%的學生說自己曾在課堂上和朋友聊天；46.9%的學生表示曾在課堂上吃東西；38.9%的學生曾在課堂上發電子郵件或做其他事情。

放學後做什麼？

　　在他們的課餘時間裏，大部分中國學生讀書或上網；大部分美國學生和朋友們一起到外面去玩；大部分日本學生進行體育活動；大部分的韓國學生看電視。

---
distracted　adj. 分心的，注意力不集中的：Ruth seemed distracted and not really interested in the meeting. 露絲似乎思想不集中，對這個會議不是很感興趣。

【參考答案】

　　1. (C)　　　　　2. (B)　　　　　3. (A)　　　　　4. (B)

Unit 16

題材　自然　　　　詞數　169　　　　建議閱讀時間　4.5 分鐘

Millions of years ago, dinosaurs lived on earth. At that time, the whole earth was warm and wet. There were great forests and they could find enough to eat.

Gradually, parts of the earth became cold and dry, and the forests there died. Then dinosaurs could not find enough to eat. This must be one reason why dinosaurs died out. There may be other reasons that we do not yet know about. Scientists are trying to make more discoveries about dinosaurs.

We now know that dinosaurs were of many sizes and shapes. Some were as small as chickens, while most were very big, some were about 90 feet long.

Some dinosaurs ate plants. Other dinosaurs ate meat. There were also terrible fights between dinosaurs! Though no man was there to see any of the fights, we can tell by the animals' footprints that showed the fights did take place.

Maybe some day you will go to the museum in your city. If you do, don't miss the Dinosaurs Room. It will be one of the biggest rooms in the museum. And there you will see the bones of the biggest animals that ever walked on land.

Millions：數百萬　dinosaur：恐龍　forest：森林　gradually：逐漸地　reason：理由
shape：形狀　footprints：腳印　museum：博物館

閱讀上面的短文，回答問題。

(　) 1. When did dinosaurs live on earth?
(A) Thousands of years ago. 　(B) Millions of months ago.
(C) Millions of years ago. 　(D) Thousands of months ago.

(　) 2. How many reasons does the writer tell us about dinosaurs' dying out?
(A) One. 　(B) Two 　(C) Three 　(D) Four

(　) 3. What are scientists trying to do about dinosaurs?
(A) To make more discoveries. 　(B) To study history.
(C) To stop discovery. 　(D) To grow up dinosaurs.

(　　) 4.　How can we know that dinosaurs often fought each other?
　　　　(A) Their bones tell us.　　　　(B) Their footprints tell us.
　　　　(C) The museums tell us.　　　　(D) The books tell us.

【參考譯文】

　　數百萬年前，恐龍生活在地球上。那時候整個地球溫暖潮濕，還有大片的森林，它們能找到充足的食物。

　　漸漸地，地球上的部分地區變得寒冷而乾燥，那裏的森林消失了。恐龍找不到足夠的食物。這肯定是恐龍滅絕的原因之一。可能還有其他原因，但我們至今還不清楚。科學家正努力發現有關恐龍的更多秘密。

　　我們現在知道，恐龍的大小、形狀各不相同。有些恐龍只有小雞那麼大，而大多數恐龍都非常大，有些甚至大約有 90 英尺長。

　　有些恐龍吃植物。還有些恐龍吃肉。恐龍之間也會發生可怕的戰爭！儘管沒有人親眼看到恐龍的打鬥場面，但我們能夠從這些動物的腳印中判斷出恐龍之間確實發生過戰爭。

　　也許有一天，你會去你所在城市的博物館。如果你去了，不要錯過恐龍館。它是博物館中最大的館之一。在那裏，你會看到曾經在陸地上行走過的最大動物的骨骼。

---

gradual　adj. 逐步的：It's a process of gradual development. 這是一個逐步發展的過程。
　　‖**gradually**　adv. 逐步地：After the storm things gradually got back to normal. 暴風雨過後，生活漸漸回復正常。
reason　n. 理由，原因：What are your reasons for quitting your job?你辭職的理由是什麼？
footprint　n. 腳印，足跡：A fox left footprints in the snow. 狐狸在雪地裏留下了足印。
terrible　adj. 激烈的，嚴重的：There was a terrible war between the two countries last
　　month. 上個月兩國之間發生了一場激戰。

【參考答案】

1. (C)　　　　2. (A)　　　　3. (A)　　　　4. (B)

Unit 17

題材　帆船運動　　詞數　165　　建議閱讀時間　4 分鐘

Welcome to our TV show On the Go. Today we are going to talk about an exciting sport—sailing. First let's talk to Sue, an 18-year-old girl who loves sailing.

Host: When did you start sailing, Sue?

Sue: I started sailing when I was 15 years old.

Host: Is it a difficult sport to learn?

Sue: Yes, it is more difficult than any other sport. For example, you need to learn about the wind directions and how to move the sails in the right way.

Host: How often do you go sailing?

Sue: I go sailing with my father every weekend.

Host: How far do you go sailing?

Sue: It depends on the wind.

Host: OK. Thank you, Sue. Good luck with your sailing.

Are you interested in sailing after hearing the interview?

If you want to learn sailing, here is a chance for you. The Water Sports Center will organize sailing lessons. Each lesson will cost you £20 and there are 5 lessons altogether.

> exciting：令人興奮的　sailing：帆船運動　direction：方向　depends on：依賴
> interview：訪談　chance：機會　organize：組織　altogether：全部

閱讀上面的短文，選擇正確答案。

(　) 1. What does Sue think of learning sailing?

A. Easy.　　　　B. Boring.　　　　C. Dangerous.　　D. Difficult.

(　) 2. Which of the following is true according to the passage?

A. Sue always sails very far.

B. Sue goes sailing with her friends.

C. Sue goes sailing every weekend.

D. Sue started sailing at the age of 18.

(　　) 3.　If you want to learn sailing at the Water Sports Center, how much will you pay?

A. £15.　　　　B. £20.　　　　C. £50.　　　　D. £100.

◖參考譯文◗

　　歡迎來到我們的電視節目《忙不停》。今天，我們要討論一項令人興奮的運動——帆船。首先，讓我們採訪一下蘇，她是一名熱愛帆船運動的 18 歲女孩。

主持人：你是什麼時候開始帆船運動的，蘇？

蘇：我是 15 歲時開始帆船運動的。

主持人：這項運動難學嗎？

蘇：是的，比任何其他運動都難學。比如你必須學會辨識風向，掌握怎樣將帆轉向正確的方向。

主持人：你多長時間練習一次？

蘇：我每個週末都和父親一起練習。

主持人：你們航行多遠？

蘇：視風的情況而定。

主持人：好的。謝謝你，蘇。祝你在帆船運動中一切順利。

　　聽了上面的採訪，你對帆船運動產生興趣了嗎？

　　如果你想學習帆船運動，現在就有機會。水上運動中心將組織帆船課。每節課收費 20 英磅，共 5 節課。

---

on the go　忙個不停：Her children kept her on the go all day. 孩子們令她整天忙個不停。

sail　n. 帆：The ship was in full sail. 這艘船的帆全都揚了起來。

◖參考答案◗

1. (D)　　　　2. (C)　　　　3. (D)

Unit 18

題材　朋友與周圍的人　　詞數　178　　建議閱讀時間　4.5 分鐘

Ron is ten years old. He loves to watch TV. But for one full year, he did not watch TV at all. What was the reason? Ron's parents said they would give him $600 if he didn't watch TV for a year.

Ron's parents thought he watched too much TV. One day his mother saw a newspaper story about a boy who didn't watch TV for a year. She showed the story to Ron. Ron liked the idea. He turned off the TV right away, and said, "It doesn't bother me not to watch TV. I just want the money."

At first, Ron's parents were very happy. Ron read books and newspapers, played outside, played computer games, and played cards with his mother. But after some time, he got bored. Every evening, he asked his parents, "What are we doing tonight?" Sometimes his mother and father wished he would watch TV just for one evening. Ron always said, "No, it would cost me money!"

Finally the year was over. Then Ron started watching his favorite TV shows all day long again. Ron got the money from his parents. What does he plan to do with the $600? "I want to buy myself a TV set!" he said.

---

bother：使人困擾　computer：電腦　bored：無趣的　Finally：終於　favorite：喜愛的
cost：花掉

閱讀上面的短文，選擇正確答案。

(　　) 1.　Ron didn't watch TV for one year because _____.
　　　　A. he wanted the money
　　　　B. watching TV too much is bad
　　　　C. he wanted to learn from the boy
　　　　D. he wanted to study harder

(　　) 2.　"*It doesn't bother me not to watch TV.*" means "It's _____ to watch TV".
　　　　A. a waste of time　　　　B. no use
　　　　C. important for me　　　　D. not important for me

（　）3.　Ron thought ＿＿＿＿ for him to read and play all the time.
　　　　　A. it was great fun　　　　　　B. it was no fun
　　　　　C. it was enjoyable　　　　　　D. it was good

（　）4.　Ron's last words would ＿＿＿＿ his parents.
　　　　　A. please　　　B. frighten　　　C. surprise　　　D. excite

【參考譯文】

　　羅恩現在 10 歲。他喜歡看電視。但有整整一年時間，他一點兒都沒有看。這是怎麼回事？羅恩的父母說，如果他在一年之內不看電視，他們就給他 600 美元。

　　羅恩的父母認爲他看電視過多。一天，他母親看到了報紙上的一個故事，故事說一個男孩一年沒有看電視。她把這個故事給羅恩看。羅恩也喜歡這個創意。他立刻關掉電視，並說：「看不看電視對我來說無所謂。我只想要錢。」

　　一開始，羅恩的父母很高興。羅恩讀書看報、去戶外玩耍、玩電腦遊戲、和母親打牌。但過了一段時間，他就覺得無聊了。每天晚上他都要問父母：「今天晚上我們幹什麼？」有時候他的父母眞希望他能看上一晚電視。但羅恩總是說：「不行，這要花我的錢！」

　　最後，一年的時間到了。這時，羅恩又開始整天看他最喜愛的電視節目了。羅恩從他父母那裏拿到了錢。他打算用這 600 美元幹什麼呢？「我想給自己買一台電視！」他說。

---

card　n. 卡片；紙牌：I never win at cards. 玩牌我總輸。
bother　v. 使煩心，煩擾：You don't look very happy. Is something bothering you?你好像不是很開心，到底有什麼事使你心煩？
cost　v. 花費：The work cost them much time. 這件工作花去他們很多時間。

【參考答案】

1. (A)　　　　2. (D)　　　　3. (B)　　　　4. (C)

Unit 19

題材 終身學習　　**詞數** 196　　**建議閱讀時間** 5分鐘

When you finish high school or university, is learning done? The answer is "no". In many countries, people continue learning all their lives. Why is lifelong learning important? How can it help you? Let's look at one example of lifelong learning in Japan.

Why is lifelong learning important?

You go to school and learn. You take tests. But learning doesn't only happen in school. And learning doesn't stop when you graduate from high school or college. You are learning all the time. For example, learning can happen when you go to a museum. It can also happen when you get a job. You learn when you play a sport or when you take a trip. Learning is life! We never stop learning. Every day, you can improve yourself by learning something new.

Lifelong learning in Japan

In Japan, lifelong learning is very important. People in Japan like to try new learning activities. Music, calligraphy, flower arranging, and foreign languages are some of their favorite classes. The Japanese take classes to improve their skills and learn new things.

Conclusion

When we graduate from school, we can continue to learn. Make lifelong learning one of your goals!

---
university：大學　lifelong：終身　graduate：畢業　college：學院；大學　trip：旅行
improve：改善　calligraphy：書法　flower arranging：插花　foreign：外國的

閱讀上面的短文，選擇正確答案。

(　　) 1. Why is lifelong learning important?

　　　　　A. It helps you improve yourself. B. It's the best way to learn.

　　　　　C. It's an important goal.　　　　D. It's fun and easy.

(　　) 2. Some people in Japan take foreign language classes to _____.

　　　　　A. get a job　　　　　　　　B. get good grades

　　　　　C. learn new things　　　　　D. finish college

(　　) 3. Which of the following is true according to the passage?

A. Learning only happens in school.

B. When we graduate from school, learning is done.

C. You can't learn anything when you play a sport.

D. Music, calligraphy, flower arranging and foreign languages are popular classes in Japan.

(　　) 4. What is the main idea of the reading?

A. Learning can be fun.

B. We are always learning in school.

C. Finishing high school is important.

D. People can learn all their lives.

【參考譯文】

當你高中或大學畢業時，學習結束了嗎？答案是「不」。在很多國家，人們一生都在不斷學習。為什麼終身學習如此重要？它對你又有怎樣的幫助？讓我們看看日本的一個終身學習的例子。

為什麼終身學習很重要？

你去學校學習，參加考試。然而，學習並不只發生在學校。而且，高中或大學畢業並不意味著學習的結束。你無時無刻不在學習。比如，去博物館時，你可以學習；找到一份工作，你也可以從中學習；從事體育運動或旅行時你也在學習。學習就是生活！我們從來都不曾停止學習。每天，你都可以通過學習新東西不斷改善自己。

日本的終身學習

在日本，終身學習是很重要的。日本人喜歡學習新鮮事物。音樂、書法、插花和外語是他們最喜歡的幾門課程。日本人通過上課來提高自身的技能，掌握新鮮事物。

結論

當我們從學校畢業時，可以繼續學習。讓終身學習成為你的目標之一。

---

calligraphy　n. 書法：He possessed astonishing skill in calligraphy. 他有驚人的書法技巧。

flower arranging　n. 插花

【參考答案】

1. (A)　　　　2. (C)　　　　3. (D)　　　　4. (D)

Unit 20

題材 戒煙　　　詞數 272　　　建議閱讀時間 7分鐘

Dear Dad,

I'm writing to you because it's too difficult to talk about it. I can't stop thinking about my uncle and how he died. In fact, I seriously want to ask you to stop smoking. I've looked up a lot of information about smoking and I have found out some disturbing things.

You already know that smoking is bad for your breathing and can cause cancer. __1__ Did you know that over 100,000 people die from smoking every year in Britain? It's the second biggest cause of death in the world. I don't want you to be one of those people.

When Mum asks you to smoke outside, you think she's annoyed. Well, it's true that she doesn't like the smell of smoke in the house and on our clothes. __2__ However, when you smoke, it's also bad for me and Mum. In other words, when we breathe in your smoke, it's like we're smoking ourselves. __3__ Doctors are finding that more and more non-smokers are falling ill because of the effects of other people's smoking.

I know that it's very difficult to stop smoking but you mustn't give in to it. Please see the doctor and ask him for help. We will do anything we can to help you. __4__ You are important to us and we don't want to lose you. Who else can I ask to help me with my maths homework or fix my bike? Please don't smoke!

Your loving daughter,

Kate

> seriously：認真地　disturbing：打擾　already：已經　breathing：呼吸　cancer：癌症
> causes：引起　annoyed：激怒　However：然而　As a result：結果　disease：疾病
> effects：效果　give in to：向…投降　fix：修理好

從下列句子中選擇最適合的答案填入：

A. As a result, we can also get diseases.

B. We are happy that you go out to smoke.

C. You must try to save your own life.

D. I've learnt that it causes many other illnesses as well.

E. It's not very pleasant.

【參考譯文】

親愛的爸爸：

　　我給你寫信是因為很難跟你當面討論。我經常忍不住想起我的叔叔和他的死因。實際上，我非常想勸你戒煙。我已經查了許多和吸煙有關的資料，也發現了一些令人擔憂的情況。

　　你已經知道吸煙對呼吸系統有害，還可能引發癌症。我發現吸煙還能引發許多其他疾病。你知道英國每年有 10 多萬人死於吸煙嗎？它是世界上第二大死因。我不想讓你成為其中的一員。

　　當媽媽讓你到外面去抽煙時，你認為她被你激怒了。她確實不喜歡房間和衣服上煙的味道。它讓人很不愉快。然而，當你抽煙時，它也對媽媽和我有害。換句話說，我們吸進了你的煙，就好像我們自己在抽煙一樣。所以，我們也會得病。醫生發現，越來越多的不吸煙者也生病了，這是被其他人抽煙影響的後果。

　　我知道戒煙很難，但你不能再向它屈服了。去看醫生吧，向他尋求幫助。我們將竭盡所能幫助你。你必須盡力挽救自己的生命。你對我們很重要，我們不想失去你。沒有了你，我還能找誰幫我完成數學家庭作業，我還能找誰幫我修自行車呢？請不要再吸煙了！

愛你的女兒
凱特

---

disturbing　adj. 令人不安的，使人苦惱的：It's very disturbing, the way they're getting rid of older employees. 他們解雇老員工的方式讓人不安。

annoyed　adj. 煩惱的，生氣的：He got very annoyed with me about my carelessness. 我的粗心大意讓他很生氣。

as well 另外，還，也：She can ride a horse and swim; she can shoot as well. 她會騎馬和游泳，另外她還會射擊。

give in 投降，認輸，屈服：We mustn't give in to threats. 我們不應屈服於威脅。

【參考答案】

　　1. (D)　　　　2. (E)　　　　3. (A)　　　　4. (C)

Unit 21

題材 地理　　詞數 222　　建議閱讀時間 5.5 分鐘

Canberra is the capital of Australia. It is a modern and lively city with a population of over 345,000.

History　Canberra is the eighth largest city in Australia. It is 238 km from Sydney and 507 km from Melbourne. Melbourne was once the capital of Australia. Sydney people also wanted to make their city the capital. It was difficult for the government to make the decision. Then in 1911, the government chose a place to build the new capital. It was between Sydney and Melbourne, the two largest cities in Australia. It took more than 14 years to build the city. In 1927, the city was set up. It became the capital and was named Canberra. "Canberra" means "a place for friends to get together."

Culture　Canberra is a beautiful city with trees and flowers everywhere. There's a Flower Festival in September each year. People can enjoy all kinds of beautiful flowers and welcome the spring to arrive. A man-made lake—Lake Burley Griffin is in the center of the city. It's about 25 km long. People like to ride bikes, walk or run around the lake. In Canberra, there're many famous universities like the Australian National University and the University of Canberra. The National Library and the National Museum of Australia are also famous places that people like to visit.

---
capital：首都　Australia：澳洲　population：人口　Sydney：雪梨　Melbourne：墨爾本
decision：決定　government：政府　Festival：慶典

閱讀上面的短文，選擇正確答案。

(　　) 1.　How far is Melbourne from Sydney?
　　　　A. 269 km.　　　B. 238 km.　　　C. 507 km.　　　D. 745 km.

(　　) 2.　The word "**Canberra**" means _____.
　　　　A. the largest city　　　　　　　B. the old capital city
　　　　C a beautiful man-made lake　　　D. a place for friends to get together

(　　) 3.　Canberra Flower Festival is a festival to _____.
　　　　A. ride bikes　　　　　　　　　B. visit universities
　　　　C. welcome the spring　　　　　　D. walk around the lake

◖參考譯文◗

坎培拉是澳洲的首都。它是一座充滿活力的現代化城市，人口超過 345,000。

歷史　坎培拉是澳大利亞第 8 大城市，距雪梨 238 公里，距墨爾本 507 公里。墨爾本曾經是澳大利亞的首都。雪梨人也想把他們的城市變成首都。政府難以作出決定。於是在 1911 年，政府選擇了一處地點建設新首都，此地位於雪梨和墨爾本——澳大利亞最大的兩座城市之間。1927 年，這座城市建成了。它成為首都，並被命名為坎培拉。「坎培拉」的意思是「朋友相聚的地方」。

文化　坎培拉是一座美麗的城市，到處綠樹成蔭、繁花似錦。每年的 9 月有一個鮮花節。人們欣賞各種美麗的鮮花，迎接春天的到來。一座人工湖——伯利·格裏芬湖位於市中心。它長約 25 公里。人們喜歡環湖騎自行車、散步或跑步。坎培拉有多所著名大學，如澳大利亞國立大學和坎培拉大學。澳大利亞國家圖書館和國家博物館也是人們喜歡遊覽的名勝。

◖參考答案◗

　　1. (D)　　　　2. (D)　　　　3. (C)

Unit 22

題材 寄宿家庭　　**詞數** 202　　**建議閱讀時間** 5 分鐘

五位學生要去英國留學，他們想要找寄宿家庭。請仔細閱讀第 1~5 題中的學生個人情況說明，並從 A~F 六個選項中幫助他們選擇最合適的寄宿家庭（其中一項為多餘選項）。

1. Zhang Chao likes Chinese food. He hopes his host family speak a little Chinese.

2. Li Wei likes doing sports. He wants to live near a park.

3. Liu Yong hopes to live near his school—Reading School. He prefers a bedroom with a bathroom.

4. Chen Yao wants to live in a big bedroom cheaper than £350 a month. She can't stand pets.

5. Hu Mei loves pets. She would like a bedroom cheaper than £220 a month.

A	B	C
Host family: The Browns Nationality: English Address: 16 Church Road (near Reading School) Room: Small, with a bathroom Price: £280/month	Host family: The Johnsons Nationality: English Address:10Shinfield Road Near Wallen School Room: Small Price: £280/month	Host family: Wang Lin Nationality: Chinese Address:48Queen's Road Room: Small Price: £230/month Other information: Good at cooking Chinese food
D	E	F
Host family: The Kings Nationality: English Address:75Erleigh Road Room: Big Price: £300/month	Host family: Judy Nationality: English Address: 6 King's Road Room: Small Price: £210/month Other information: A pet dog	Host family: The Rays Nationality: English Address: 22 Wokingham Road(near Palmer Park) Room: Big Price: £370/month

◖參考譯文◗

1. 張超喜歡中餐，他希望寄宿家庭能說一點國語。
2. 李威喜歡運動，他想住在公園附近。
3. 劉勇希望住在自己就讀的學校——語言學校附近，他想要一間帶浴室的臥室。
4. 陳瑤想住月租金低於 350 英鎊的大臥室。她接受不了寵物。
5. 胡玫喜歡寵物，她想要一間租金低於每月 220 英鎊的臥室。

A	B	C
寄宿家庭：布朗家 國籍：英國 地址：教堂路 16 號(靠近語言學校) 房間：小,有浴室 價格：每月 280 英鎊	寄宿家庭：約翰遜家 國籍：英國 地址：欣菲爾德路 10 號靠近沃倫學校 房間：小 價格：每月 280 英鎊	寄宿家庭：王林 國籍：中國 地址：皇后路 48 號 房間：小 價格：每月 230 英鎊 其他資訊：擅長烹飪中餐
D	**E**	**F**
寄宿家庭：金家 國籍：英國 地址：厄利路 75 號 房間：大 價格：每月 300 英鎊	寄宿家庭：朱迪 國籍：英國 地址：國王路 6 號 房間：小 價格：每月 210 英鎊 其他資訊：有一條寵物狗	寄宿家庭：雷家 國籍：英國 地址：沃金厄姆路 22 號(靠近帕爾默公園) 房間：大 價格：每月 370 英鎊

nationality　n. 國籍：May I ask your nationality, sir? 先生，可以告訴我你的國籍嗎？

◖參考答案◗

　　1. (C)　　　　2. (F)　　　　3. (A)　　　　4. (D)　　　　5. (E)

Unit 23

題材 哲理　　　**詞數** 178　　　**建議閱讀時間** 4.5 分鐘

Once upon a time there lived a fisherman in a village near the sea. One day the fisherman set out in a small boat. After he had got to a good place for fishing, he threw a long rope with many hooks into the water. Before he had finished doing it, it became very heavy. He thought it seemed too heavy to be a fish, and began to draw in the rope.

When the hooks came out of the water, he was surprised, for the hooks were holding some golden chains. When he pulled them, more and more golden chains came out. Soon there was a large pile of the golden chains in his boat.

"I shall be very rich," he said to himself, "I can sell the chains for a lot of money. With the money I shall buy a new boat and some new nets. I shall build a house. I shall be the richest man in the world." He went on pulling. He felt so pleased that he did not notice what was happening to his boat. It began to sink. He lost not only all the golden chains but also his boat and his life.

---

village：村莊　threw：扔(throw 的過去式)　rope：繩子　hook：鉤子　chains：鍊子
pile：堆　notice：注意　sink：下沉

閱讀上面的短文，選擇正確答案。

(　) 1. The fisherman began to pull the rope _____.
　　　A. when there was a fish　　　B. after he finished throwing it
　　　C. when it became very heavy　　D. when he saw the golden chains

(　) 2. It was so heavy that the fisherman thought _____.
　　　A. it must be a lot of stones　　B. it could not be a fish
　　　C. it must be a lot of grass　　　D. it must be a fish

(　) 3. To his surprise, _____
　　　A. there was a lot of shoes on the hooks
　　　B. there was a large pile of golden chains in his boat
　　　C. there were some golden chains on the hooks
　　　D. he caught a very big fish

(　　) 4. The fisherman said to himself that _____.

   A. he would give his wife a present

   B. he would buy a new boat and some new nets

   C. he would buy a house

   D. he would marry a young girl

(　　) 5. He did not notice the boat began to sink because _____.

   A. he was thinking of money and was too happy

   B. he was very tired

   C. he went on pulling the hooks

   D. he didn't mind what to happen

【參考譯文】

　　從前，在海邊的村子裏住著一個漁夫。一天，漁夫乘小船出海。當他來到一個捕魚的好地方後，他向水中撒下一根帶有很多鉤子的長繩子。在他完全撒完之前，繩子已經變得很重了。他想，繩子太重，釣到的似乎不是魚，他開始拉繩子。

　　當鉤子露出水面後，他驚呆了，因為鉤子上掛著一些金鍊子。當他往上拉時，越來越多的金鍊子露了出來。很快，一大堆金鍊子堆在了船上。

　　「我要發大財了，」他自言自語道，「我可以把這些鏈子賣掉，換回很多錢。有了這些錢，我可以買一條新船和一些新漁網。我再蓋幢房子。我就是世界上最富有的人了。」他不停地拉。他開心極了，沒有注意到他的船正在發生變化。船開始沉沒。他不僅失去了所有的金鍊子，也失去了船和自己的性命。

---

hook n.（魚）鉤 v. 用鉤釣起：The fisherman hooked three trout in the stream. 那位漁夫從溪水裏釣到 3 條鱒魚。

chain n. 鏈條，手鏈，項鍊：She was wearing a silver chain round her neck. 她戴著銀項鍊。

pile n. 堆，疊：He always left his books in a neat pile. 他總是把書疊得整整齊齊的。

net n. 網：fishing nets 漁網/a butterfly net 捕蝶網/a tennis net 網球網/a hair net 護髮網罩/a mosquito net 蚊帳

notice v. 注意到，覺察到：We noticed a car stopping outside the house. 我們看見一輛轎車在那房子外面停下來。

【參考答案】

 1. (C)   2. (B)   3. (C)   4. (B)   5. (A)

Unit 24

| 題材 | 朋友與周圍的人 | 詞數 | 154 | 建議閱讀時間 | 4 分鐘 |

▶Mrs. Reeser was a teacher for 32 years. When she stopped teaching, she decided to do some things that she had never done before. One thing she wanted to do was learn how to fly.

After taking flying lessons for a few hours, Mrs. Reeser had another idea—she wanted to jump out of an airplane. She put on a parachute, opened the plane's door, and leaped. Down she floated. At the time she jumped from the plane, Mrs. Reeser was 61 years old.

▶For many years Bill Port had a great job—he liked it and so did his customers. If your bicycle broke down, you just had to call Bill. Bill would go to your house and repair your bike.

Bill had a truck that carried 18,000 bicycle parts and all his tools. When someone called to have a bike fixed, Bill drove to the house and fixed it right away.

Bill has retired from his mobile bike repair business. Perhaps you'd like to take his place.

> parachute：降落傘　leap：往前跳　float：漂浮　customers：顧客　repair：修理　truck：貨車　fix：修理　mobile：移動

閱讀上面的短文，選擇正確答案。

(　) 1.　Mrs. Reeser was a teacher for _____.
　　　　A. a few hours　B. 32 years　　　C. 60 years　　　D. 50 years

(　) 2.　When Mrs. Reeser jumped, she wore _____.
　　　　A. wings　　　　B. a kite　　　　C. a parachute　D. large shoes

(　) 3.　You can tell from the story that Mrs. Reeser likes to _____.
　　　　A. stay at home　　　　　　　B. drive race cars
　　　　C. try new things　　　　　　D. plant flowers

(　) 4.　Bill carried his tools in _____.
　　　　A. his pocket　B. a truck　　　C. a bag　　　　D. his hat

(　　) 5. The story says that Bill Port _____.

      A. was very tall   B. hated children

      C. fixed bicycles   D. fixed trucks

(　　) 6. You can tell that Bill Port _____.

      A. lost customers   B. had a helper

      C. went to school   D. was prepared to fix bicycles

【參考譯文】

▶李瑟太太教書 32 年。退休後，她決定做一些以前從未做過的事。其中之一是學開飛機。

在學了幾個小時的飛行課程後，李瑟太太有了其他想法——她想從飛機上跳下來。她背上降落傘，打開艙門，縱身一躍，飄蕩而下。她從飛機上跳下的時候，已經 61 歲了。

▶許多年來，比爾·波特一直在從事一項偉大的工作——他喜歡這個工作，他的顧客也是如此。如果你的自行車壞了，只要給比爾打個電話。他會上門為你修車。

比爾有一輛卡車，上面裝著 18,000 個自行車零配件，還有他的全部工具。只要有人打電話請他修車，他就會開車來到那人家裏，立刻把車修好。

比爾已經退休，不再幹流動修車這一行了。也許你想接替他的位置吧。

---

parachute n. 降落傘：a backpack parachute 背包式降落傘

leap   v. 跳，躍：When the bus slowed down, the men leaped off. 公共汽車慢下來後，男人們跳下了車。

float   v. 漂浮；飄浮：The feather floated lightly in the air. 羽毛輕盈地飄在空中。

【參考答案】

1. (B)   2. (C)   3. (C)   4. (B)   5. (C)

6. (D)

Unit 25

題材 家庭、朋友與周圍的人　　詞數 155　　建議閱讀時間 4分鐘

　　Mr. Robertson was the owner of a large company. One day he went into his office early in the morning to get ready to go to the airport. He was leaving his office when Bill, a night watchman, came in. Bill just came off work. After saying "Good morning" to Mr. Robertson, Bill told the owner about his bad dream: last night he dreamed Mr. Robertson's plane crashed soon after take-off. Hearing this, Mr. Robertson was surprised. He decided to go by land.

　　Bill's dream came true. That morning the plane really crashed just after it had taken off. Later Mr. Robertson returned to his office and heard the accident. To express his thanks, Mr. Robertson gave Bill 5,000 dollars with a letter. Mr. Robertson told Bill that he was dismissed. Bill was surprised and asked why. Mr. Robertson said, "Go home and read the letter, and you'll know."

　　Bill went home and opened the letter in a hurry. After reading it, he became very sad. In the letter there was only one sentence. Can you guess what?

---
owner：擁有者　company：公司　watchman：警衛　crash：墜毀　express：表達
dismissed：被革職　hurry：匆忙

閱讀上面的短文，選擇正確答案。

(　　) 1.　The night watchman _____.
　　　　A. worked very hard　　　　B. had a terrible dream
　　　　C. wasn't kind to Mr. Robertson　D. saw a plane crash

(　　) 2.　When he was told the dream, Mr. Robertson was very _____.
　　　　A. sad　　　　C. pleased　　　　C. worried　　　　D. surprised

(　　) 3.　When Bill opened the letter, he knew _____.
　　　　A. he was dismissed
　　　　B. why he was dismissed
　　　　C. he had got $5,000
　　　　D. Mr. Robertson thanked him very much

(　　) 4. The sentence in the letter could be "_____".

    A. I don't want you to work here any longer because you have saved me once

    B. I don't want to see you again because of your terrible dream

    C. A night watchman should keep awake the whole night

    D. Thanks a lot for telling me your dream

【參考譯文】

　　羅伯遜先生是一家大公司的老闆，一天，他早早來到辦公室，準備去機場。正當他要離開辦公室時，守夜人比爾走了進來。比爾剛下班。在跟羅伯遜先生說了句「早安」後，比爾告訴老闆說，自己做了一個夢：昨天晚上他夢見羅伯遜先生的飛機起飛不久即墜毀。聽到這裏，羅伯遜先生很吃驚。他決定搭車過去。

　　比爾的夢應驗了。那天早上，飛機確實是剛剛起飛就墜毀了。羅伯遜先生返回辦公室後，聽說了這件事。爲了表達他的謝意。羅伯遜先生用信封裝了 5,000 美元送給比爾。同時告訴他，他被解雇了。比爾很吃驚，問爲什麼。羅伯遜先生說，「回家看看信，你就會明白的。」

　　比爾趕忙回家打開信。讀完後，他很難過。信裏面只有一句話，你能猜出是什麼嗎？

---

own　v. 擁有 ‖ **owner**　n. 擁有者，物主，老闆

watch　v. 注視，看，監視 ‖ **watchman**　n. 看守人，警衛員

come off　結束，完成：come off work 下班

crash　v. （飛機等）墜毀：The plane crashed in the mountains. 飛機在山中墜毀。

express　v. （用言詞、表情、行動）表達：She expressed surprise when I told her how much it was. 當我告訴她這東西多少錢時，她表現出驚訝的神情。

dismiss　v. 解雇，開除：I was dismissed for being late. 我因遲到而被解雇。

guess　v. 猜測，推測：I guessed the answer to the math problem. 我猜對了那道數學題的答案。

【參考答案】

  1. (B)　　　　2. (D)　　　　3. (B)　　　　4. (C)

Unit 26

題材　美國鄉村音樂　　詞數　202　　建議閱讀時間　5 分鐘

Western country music is very old. It came from the United States, Canada, Ireland, and Great Britain. It is a mixture of music from all of these places.

In the west of America, cowboys had to __1__ the cattle. They had to watch them all day and all night because the cattle were nervous and sometimes ran away. A cowboy's life was lonely and dangerous. When he was alone in the desert with the cattle, he drank strong coffee to stay awake at night. __2__ Of course, the cowboys also sang music when they traveled to town to relax and have a good time.

In the south of America, many people came from Ireland, Scotland, and England. Other people came from France, Canada. They enjoyed their own kind of music. When they visited their friends and families on holidays like Thanksgiving and Christmas, they usually sang and played country music.

__3__ It talks about love, jobs, home and money. It talks about friends and enemies, farms and crops. People in many parts of the world like western country music because everyone knows something about these ideas.

---

mixture：混合體　cowboys：牛仔　nervous：緊張的　lonely：寂寞的　desert：沙漠　relax：休閒　describes：描述　crops：莊稼

閱讀上面的短文，選擇正確答案。

(　) 1.　A. take care of　　　　　B. look forward to
　　　　　C. think much of　　　　D. keep away from

(　) 2.　A. He also gave some coffee to the cattle to make them awake.
　　　　　B. He also slept with the cattle for a long time.
　　　　　C. He also kept the cattle awake to keep off the enemy.
　　　　　D. He also sang music to the cattle to make them quiet.

(　) 3.　A. Western country music describes cattle.
　　　　　B. Western country music describes life.
　　　　　C. Western country music describes desert.
　　　　　D. Western country music describes countries.

【參考譯文】

　　美國西部鄉村音樂非常古老。它來自美國、加拿大、愛爾蘭和英國，是所有這些地方音樂的混合體。

　　在美國西部，牛仔必須照顧牛。他們必須沒日沒夜地照顧它們，因為牛很膽小，有時候會到處亂跑。牛仔的生活是孤獨而危險的。當他獨自一人和牛群待在沙漠裏時，他會喝濃咖啡來熬夜。他也會給牛唱歌來讓它們安靜。當然，當牛仔們來到城鎮休息或玩耍的時候，他們也會唱歌。

　　在美國南部，許多人來自愛爾蘭、蘇格蘭和英格蘭。其他人來自法國和加拿大。他們喜歡自己的音樂。當他們在感恩節或聖誕節之類的假期拜訪朋友和家人時，他們通常都要唱歌並演奏鄉村音樂。

　　西部鄉村音樂描寫生活，談論愛情、工作、家庭和金錢。它也談論朋友和敵人、農場和莊稼。世界上許多地方的人都喜歡西部鄉村音樂，因為大家對他們的思想多少有些瞭解。

---

mixture　n. 混合，混合體：People are a mixture of good and evil. 人集善惡於一身。
Thanksgiving　n. 感恩節（美國 11 月份的一個公共假日）

【參考答案】

　　1. (A)　　　　2. (D)　　　　3. (B)

Unit 27

題材　健康　　　　詞數　163　　　　建議閱讀時間　4分鐘

Hello, listeners. Welcome to Henton Hospital Radio. Before our music program at four, I'm going to repeat some of our hospital rules.

The hospital can hold 800 patients. There're 8 beds in each ward. The visiting hours are in the afternoon from 2:30 to 3:30 and in the evening from 7:00 to 8:00. But remember only two people can see you at the same time. Sorry about that, but you can see what would happen if we didn't have these rules.

The other rules are about our hours. We start quite early—you might not be used to that. We wake you at 6 o'clock, and breakfast is at 8 o'clock, lunch is at noon. There's tea at 3:30 and supper is at 6 o'clock.

You can see the sign "no smoking"—we don't allow smoking in the wards. I'm sure you understand why. However, if you do need to smoke, there are some smoking-rooms.

You will find the radio switch on the wall near your bed, with your own headphones, if you want to listen. It's our own hospital radio wishing you a quick recovery.

---

repeat：重複　ward：病房　allow：允許　switch：開關　headphones：頭戴式耳機
recovery：康復

閱讀上面的短文，回答問題。

(　) 1. What is not allowed in the wards?
A. talking 　　　B. smoking 　　　C. drinking 　　　D. sleeping

(　) 2. Who do you think the listeners might be?
A. doctors 　　　B. patients 　　　C. nurses 　　　D. guests

(　) 3. How many wards are there in this hospital?
A. 80 　　　　　B. 90 　　　　　C. 100 　　　　　D. 110

(　) 4. Where can the patients smoke?
A. outside the hospital 　　　　B. in the hall
C. smoking-rooms 　　　　　　D. restaurants

(　　) 5. What program will follow this radio talk?
  A. a music program
  B. a talk show
  C. a movie
  D. a news time

【參考譯文】

聽眾朋友，你們好。歡迎收聽亨頓醫院的廣播。在下午4點的音樂節目之前，我要重複一下我們醫院的部分院規。

醫院能容納800名病人。每間病房有8張床位。探視時間是下午2點半到3點半和晚上7點到8點。但請記住，一次只能有兩人探視。對此我們很抱歉，但你們也明白，如果我們不這麼辦，會有什麼後果。

其他守則是關於時間安排的。我們起床很早——你可能不太適應。我們將在6點鐘叫醒你，早飯時間是8點，午飯時間在中午。3點半是下午茶時間，晚飯安排在6點。

你能看到「禁煙」的標誌——病房裏不准吸煙。我想你們肯定明白其中的原因。然而，如果你確實很想抽，我們這裏有吸煙室。

你會發現收音機的按鈕在靠床的牆上，如果你想聽，還有獨立使用的耳機。這是我們醫院自己的廣播節目，希望你能儘快康復。

---

ward　n. 病房：Hospital wards are usually very clean places. 醫院的病房通常很乾淨。
wake　v. 叫醒，喚醒：Please wake me up at 8 o'clock. 請在八點鐘叫醒我。
allow　v. 允許：His father allows him to drive the car. 他父親允許他開這輛車。
switch　n. 開關：Somebody pressed the wrong switch. 有人按錯了開關。
recover　v. 恢復（健康，知覺等）‖**recovery**　n. 痊癒，康復：They wished him a quick recovery. 他們祝願他早日恢復健康。

【參考答案】

1. (B)　　2. (B)　　3. (C)　　4. (C)　　5. (A)

Unit 28

題材　社會　　　詞數　129　　　建議閱讀時間　3分鐘

Dear editor,

Can't your newspaper do something about the custom of hitchhiking?

A short time ago, on a car travel I counted at least 50 people standing beside the road, asking for rides. Many of them were young women.

Don't they understand how dangerous it is to get into the car driven by a stranger? How much do they know about the driver? Is he a good driver or not? Nothing!

Many of these young hitchhikers may come from good families. Don't their parents teach them anything about the world? I always taught my children not to talk to strangers. I never let them take rides from people they didn't know.

Isn't there enough crime today? Don't ask for trouble by hitchhiking again. On the other hand, hitchhiking may bring some traffic trouble.

Don't you think what I said is true?

A worried grandfather

---

editor：編輯　custom：習慣　hitchhiking：搭便車　count：計算　crime：犯罪
traffic：交通　worried：擔憂的

閱讀上面的短文，選擇正確答案。

(　　) 1. The Worried Grandfather _____.
    A. doesn't like young women to drive cars
    B. thinks it is dangerous for a young woman to get into a stranger's car
    D. never lets his children get into other people's car
    D. likes drivers to be careful and strict in their work

(　　) 2. The Worried Grandfather _____.
    A. was hit by a car when he was standing by the road
    B. is in trouble now and he wants to get some help from the newspaper
    C. is a good driver and often gives free rides to strangers
    D. has seen much of the world and he is very careful

（　　）3. The Worried Grandfather wrote the letter to tell _____.

　　　　A. the newspaper to let its readers know the danger of hitchhiking

　　　　B. young women never to go on a long travel alone

　　　　C. young people to listen to their parents at home

　　　　D. his children not to talk to strangers on the road

（　　）4. What do you think a good editor is going to do after he receives the letter?

　　　　A. He will return the letter to the old man.

　　　　B. He will give the letter to the police station.

　　　　C. He will write something about the danger of hitchhiking in the newspaper.

　　　　D. He will hold a meeting to tell the drivers to make the traffic trouble less.

【參考譯文】

親愛的編輯：

　　你們的報紙不能對搭便車的習慣有所作為嗎？

　　不久前，我開車旅行，我數了一下，沿途至少有 50 個人請求搭便車。其中許多都是女孩子。

　　難道她們不知道坐進陌生人駕駛的汽車有多危險嗎？她們對司機有多少瞭解？司機是好人還是壞人？她們一無所知！

　　這些搭便車的年輕人中可能有很多來自正經人家。難道他們的父母沒有告訴過他們這個世界是怎樣一個世界嗎？我總是教導我的孩子不要和陌生人說話。我從不讓他們搭乘不認識的人的車。

　　現在的犯罪還不夠多嗎？不要再因為搭便車給自己找麻煩了。另一方面，搭便車也可能引發交通問題。

　　難道你不覺得我說得對嗎？

一位焦慮的祖父

editor n. 編輯：She's a senior editor in a publishing company. 她是一家出版公司的高級編輯。

custom n. 習慣，風俗：It is my custom to get up early and have a cold bath every morning. 我習慣每天早晨早起並洗個冷水澡。

hitchhike v. 沿途免費搭乘便車旅行：They hitchhiked across the country. 他們搭便車穿越全國。‖**hitchhiker** n. 免費搭車者

【參考答案】

1. (B)　　　　2. (D)　　　　3. (A)　　　　4. (C)

Unit 29

題材　歷史和地理　　詞數　112　　建議閱讀時間　3分鐘

Peter the Great was a very important Russian ruler. As a child, he was smart and curious. He learned about modern science and technology. And he was very interested in boats.

After 1689, he ruled Russia on his own. He created Russia's first navy. He also made the army stronger. To learn more about modern science and technology, he traveled around Europe for 18 months. Many scientists returned with him to Russia.

In 1703, Peter built a brand-new city—St. Petersburg. It was a symbol of the new Russia. People called it "the window to the west".

Peter also brought many reforms to Russia. Education, business, politics, and the army became more modern. And he started Russia's first newspaper.

Peter made Russia a strong, modern, and powerful country. Indeed, Peter the Great changed Russia greatly!

> Russian：俄羅斯　ruler：統治者　smart：聰明的　technology：技術　create：創建
> navy：海軍　army：陸軍　brand-new：全新的　symbol：象徵　reform：改革

閱讀上面的短文，選擇正確答案。

(　) 1.　As a child, Peter _____.
　　　A. liked boats　　　　　　　B. was not very intelligent
　　　C. liked to read the newspaper　D. ruled Russia on his own

(　) 2.　What did Peter do in Europe?
　　　A. He visited his relatives.　　B. He created a navy.
　　　C. He bought a boat.
　　　D. He learned about new kinds of technology.

(　) 3.　The article doesn't talk about reforms in _____.
　　　A. business　　B. politics　　C. art　　　D. education

(　) 4.　What does the underlined word "**it**" mean?
　　　A. St. Petersburg.　　　　B. Russia.
　　　C. Europe.　　　　　　　D. Peter.

(　) 5.　What can we say about Peter the Great?
　　　　　A. He didn't do much to help Russia.
　　　　　B. He wanted to make Russia modern.
　　　　　C. He was very lazy.
　　　　　D. He didn't like to travel.

【參考譯文】

　　彼得大帝是俄國歷史上非常重要的一位統治者。當他還是個孩子的時候，就已經非常聰明而且很好奇。他學習現代的科學技術，並對船產生了濃厚的興趣。

　　從 1689 年起，他開始親自統治俄國。他創建了俄國第一支海軍。他還使陸軍更強大。為了學到更多現代的科學技術，他遊歷歐洲達 18 個月。許多科學家和他一起返回俄國。

　　1703 年，彼得建立了一座全新的城市——聖彼得堡。這座城市是新俄國的象徵。人們把它稱作「通往西方的窗口」。

　　彼得還對俄國進行了許多改革。教育、商業、政治以及軍事變得更加先進了。他還開辦了俄國第一份報紙。

　　彼得使俄國成為一個強大、先進和富有實力的國家。確實，彼得大帝極大地改變了俄國。

technology　n. 科技，技術：Modern civilization depends greatly on technology. 現代文明在很大程度上依靠工業技術的發展。

brand-new　adj. 嶄新的：How can he afford to buy himself a brand-new car? 他怎麼會有錢給自己買新車？

symbol　n. 象徵，標誌：In the picture the tree is the symbol of life. 在這幅畫中，樹是生命的象徵。

reform　n. 改革：The new law brought many social reforms. 這項新的法律帶來了許多社會改革。

【參考答案】

1. (A)　　　　2. (D)　　　　3. (C)　　　　4. (A)　　　　5. (B)

Unit 30

題材　家庭、朋友與周圍的人　　詞數　160　　建議閱讀時間　4分鐘

Dick was a painter. He painted beautiful pictures.

Once the king of England asked him to paint some pictures on the walls of the palaces. Several workers came and made a big platform. Then Dick began to paint. He worked with a man who helped him.

At the end of the year the pictures were ready. They were beautiful. Dick looked for a long time. How beautiful they were! He took one step back and looked again. Now the pictures were more beautiful. He took another step, then another, until he was at the very edge of the platform. But he didn't know it. He thought of only his pictures.

The worker who helped him saw everything. "What shall I do?" he thought. "Dick is at the very edge of the platform. If I cry out, he will take another step and will fall down to the stone floor. It will kill him." The worker quickly took a pot of paint, ran to a picture and threw the paint at the picture. "What are you doing?" the painter cried and ran to his picture.

---

palace：皇宮　several：幾個　platform：平台　edge：邊緣　pot：罐子、壺

閱讀上面的短文，選擇正確答案。

(　) 1. Dick worked _____.
　　A. with another painter　　　　B. with a worker
　　C. with several men　　　　　　D. alone

(　) 2. The painter didn't know he was in danger because _____.
　　A. he was looking at the picture
　　B. he was painting the picture
　　C. he was walking about
　　D. he was talking to the worker

(　) 3. The worker _____ to save the painter.
　　A. cried out
　　B. ran away
　　C. threw the paint at the picture
　　D. asked others

（　　）4. The painter was very _____ when the worker threw the paint at the picture.

    A. happy   B. pleased   C. sad   D. angry

（　　）5. At last, the painter _____.

    A. fell down to the floor   B. took another step

    C. was saved   D. ran away quickly

【參考譯文】

迪克是一位畫家。他畫的畫很漂亮。

有一次，英國國王讓他在宮殿的牆上作畫。幾個工人過來搭建了一座很大的平臺。迪克就在上面畫起來。他工作的時候，有一個人在旁邊幫忙。

年底的時候，畫作基本完工了。它們很漂亮。迪克欣賞了很長時間。它們真美啊！他退後一步，又看了看，這些畫似乎更美了。他又退後一步，又是一步，這時，他已到了平臺的邊緣。但他不知道。他滿腦子都是自己的畫。

協助他工作的工人看得很明白。「我該怎麼辦？」他想。「迪克已經到了平臺的最邊上。假如我大喊大叫，他會再退一步，摔到下面的石頭地面上。這樣會摔死的。」這名工人迅速拿起一罐油漆，跑到一幅畫作旁，把油漆往畫上潑。「你在幹什麼？」畫家一邊大喊，一邊跑向自己的畫作。

---

paint v. （用顏料）畫：She painted a beautiful portrait for us. 她為我們畫了一幅很美的肖像畫。‖ **painter** n. 畫家：He is a famous British water-color painter. 他是英國著名的水彩畫家。

palace n. 王宮，宮殿：Buckingham Palace 白金漢宮

platform n. 平臺，講臺，舞臺：a viewing platform 觀景平臺

pot n. 罐，缽，壺：A pot may hold food or drink or contain earth for flowers to grow in. 罐子可以盛食物或飲料，也可以填土種花。

【參考答案】

1. (B)   2. (A)   3. (C)   4. (D)   5. (C)

Unit 31

| 題材 | 能量 | 詞數 | 173 | 建議閱讀時間 | 4.5 分鐘 |

Think of all the things that move. People move their bodies. Cars __1__ along the road. Rain __2__ to the ground. But do you know what is involved in all this movement? The __3__ is energy. Energy is all around you. You will find energy in your home, in factories, at airports, and in playing fields.

Look around your home. What do you see? There are many appliances and machines. You may find a stove, a refrigerator, and a toaster in the __4__. There may be a television in the living room. There are lights in every room. Your family might also have a car and a lawn mower. All of these machines and appliances work by __5__ energy. __6__ energy, we couldn't use any of these things.

You can get energy by plugging things into electrical outlets. You can also get energy by __7__ fuels like oil and gas. There is __8__ energy in the __9__ you eat. There is energy in the sunlight that shines __10__ your windows. There is energy all around.

---
involved：包含　field：場地　appliance：(電器)設備　lawn mower：剪草機
plug：插入　electrical：電的　outlet：出口、插座　fuel：燃料

閱讀上面的短文，選擇正確答案。

( ) 1. A. jump B.ride C.cover D.drive

( ) 2. A. goes B.falls C.grows D.blows

( ) 3. A. answer B.article C.envelope D.invitation

( ) 4. A. floor B.kitchen C.window D.room

( ) 5. A. spending B.using C.taking D.keeping

( ) 6. A. Except B.Instead C.With D.Without

( ) 7. A. hurting B.burning C.cooking D.hitting

( ) 8. A. too B.also C.either D.yet

( ) 9. A. air B.medicine C.food D.water

( ) 10. A. down B.for C.towards D.through

【參考譯文】

想想所有那些可以動的東西。人移動自己的身體，汽車沿公路行駛，雨落在地上。可是你知道所有這些運動中都包含什麼嗎？答案就是能量。能量無處不在，你可以在自己的家裏、工廠、機場和遊樂場找到它們。

環顧一下自己的家，你能看到什麼？許多電器和設備。你會看到廚房裏有火爐、冰箱和烤麵包機，客廳裏有電視，每個房間都有燈。你們家可能還有汽車和割草機。所有這些設備和電器都是依靠能量工作的，沒有能量，它們就無法使用。

把插頭插進插座就能獲得能量，點燃汽油和天然氣之類的燃料也可以獲得能量，人吃的食物裏也有能量，照進窗戶的陽光也有能量。能量無處不在。

---

appliance　n. 家用設備（尤指電器）：household appliances such as dishwashers and washing machines 洗碗機、洗衣機之類的家用電器

stove　n. 爐子：There is a large pan on the stove. 爐子上有一口大平底鍋。

toast　v. 烘，烤（麵包等）：toast slices of bread for lunch 烤麵包片作午餐 ‖ **toaster**　n. 烤麵包機

lawn　n. 草坪：lawn chairs 草坪用椅

mow　v. 割：mow the grass 割草 ‖ **mower**　n. 割草機

plug　v. 插入（插座），接通（電源）：I plugged in the kettle. 我把水壺接上了電源。

outlet　n. 電源插座

【參考答案】

1. (D)	2. (B)	3. (A)	4. (B)	5. (B)
6. (D)	7. (B)	8. (B)	9. (C)	10. (D)

Unit 32

題材 朋友與周圍的人　　詞數 190　　建議閱讀時間 4.5分鐘

Two men named Jack and Joe were walking along a road one hot summer morning. They were very thirsty and wanted very much to have a glass of cold beer, but they had no money.

"I can get some beer for us without money," said Jack. "Come with me." They went to a pub about one kilometer away. It was lunch time and a lot of people were in the pub. The owner was selling drinks at one end of the long counter and a waiter was selling drinks at the other end.

"My friend and I can't agree," Jack went up to the owner and said. "I say there are two glasses in a liter and he says there are three." "You are right," said the owner, "There are only two glasses in a liter." "Thank you." said Jack, and went over to where Joe was standing at the other end of the counter.

He asked for two glasses of beer and told the waiter that the owner was going to pay for it. Then he called out loudly. "You did say two glasses, didn't you, owner?" "Yes, that's right. Two glasses." The owner called back. So they drank the beer with great enjoyment and then walked out of the pub.

pub：小酒館　counter：櫃台　enjoyment：享受

閱讀上面的短文，回答問題。

(　　) 1.　Why did they want very much to have cold beer?
　　　　A. They were happy.　　　　B. They were thirsty.
　　　　C. They were hungry.　　　　D. They were tired.

(　　) 2.　They wanted to get the beer without paying money because _____.
　　　　A. they were friends of the owner
　　　　B. there were many people in the pub
　　　　C. they had no money
　　　　D. they wanted to keep the money

(　　) 3.　There were a lot of people in the pub because _____.
　　　　A. it was lunch time　　　　B. it was very hot
　　　　C. the beer was very good there　　D. it was a good pub

(　　) 4. ＿＿＿＿ said that there were two glasses in a liter.
      A. Only Jack　　　　　　　　B. Only Joe
      C. Only the owner　　　　　　D. Jack and the owner

(　　) 5. Jack was ＿＿＿＿ than Joe.
      A. cleverer　　　B. more foolish　C. taller　　　　D. richer

【參考譯文】

　　一個炎熱的夏天上午，傑克和喬走在馬路上。他們口渴難耐，很想喝一杯冰啤酒，但他們沒有錢。

　　「我能不花錢弄些啤酒來，」傑克說。「跟我來。」他們來到大約一公里外的一家酒吧。當時正是午餐時間，酒吧裏人很多。老闆在長櫃檯的一頭，侍者在另一頭，他們都在賣酒。

　　「我和我的朋友看法不一，」傑克走向老闆說。「我說一升酒能裝兩杯，他說能裝三杯。」「你說得對，」老闆說，「一升酒只能裝兩杯。」「謝謝你，」傑克說，然後走向站在櫃檯另一頭的喬。

　　他要了兩杯啤酒，並告訴侍者老闆請客。然後大聲喊道：「你說兩杯，是吧，老闆？」「是的，沒錯。兩杯。」老闆大聲回答道。他們就這樣開開心心地喝完啤酒，然後走出酒吧。

---

pub　n. 酒吧：Keep your voice down! The whole pub can hear you. 小聲點！整個酒吧的人都聽見你的話啦。

litre　n. 升（容量單位）：ten litres of petrol 10 升汽油

enjoyment　n. 樂趣，樂事：She gets a lot of enjoyment from travelling. 旅遊帶給她無窮樂趣。

【參考答案】

    1. (B)　　　　　2. (C)　　　　　3. (A)　　　　　4. (D)　　　　　5. (A)

Unit 33

題材　人物介紹　　詞數　183　　建議閱讀時間　4.5分鐘

James Herriot was a famous doctor for animals. He was born in Scotland in 1915. He grew up with a pet dog named Don. ___1___, Don went with him. Herriot loved animals so much that ___2___ to be a vet, especially for dogs.

After he graduated from high school, he found a job in Yorkshire in England to heal large animals, such as horses, cows, sheep and pigs. Herriot loved the beautiful countryside, but treating large animals was very hard work. Before long, he found out that sick dogs there were never treated, because the vets wouldn't heal them. ___3___. At first, other vets laughed at him, for his not working on "real" animals. But the owners of the dogs were thankful to him, because they regarded the dogs as their ___4___.

Later in his life, Herriot wrote a lot about his experience in Yorkshire, England. He even wrote a book, just about dogs, James Herriot's Dog Stories. ___5___, he loved dogs the best.

vet：獸醫　graduated：畢業　heal：治療　treat：治療　regard...as...：視...為...

選擇適當的答案填入空格中：

A. he made up his mind

B. No matter how much he loved all kinds of animals

C. family members

D. Wherever he went

E. He loved dogs all his life.

F. He started treating dogs

【參考譯文】

　　詹姆斯‧赫裏奧特是一位著名的獸醫，他于 1915 年出生於蘇格蘭。他和一條名叫唐的寵物狗一起長大。不論他走到哪里，唐都跟著他。赫裏奧特非常喜歡動物，以至於他下定決心做一名獸醫，特別是給狗看病的獸醫。

　　高中畢業後，他在英格蘭的約克郡找到了一份治療大型動物的工作，這些大型動物指的是馬、牛、羊、豬等。赫裏奧特喜歡美麗的鄉村風景，但治療大型動物是非常艱苦的活。不久，他就發現那裏的狗生病了卻得不到醫治，因爲獸醫不肯給它們看病。他開始爲狗治病。一開始，其他獸醫都嘲笑他，因爲他治療的不是「正經」動物。但狗的主人很感激他，因爲他們認爲狗是家庭的一員。

　　在他生命的後期，赫裏奧特寫了許多自己在英格蘭約克郡的經歷。他甚至寫了本書，就是關於狗的，書名叫做《詹姆斯‧赫裏奧特的狗的故事》。儘管他熱愛所有的動物，他的最愛還是狗。

---

vet　n. 獸醫：Get you kitten checked by the vet. 讓獸醫給你的小貓檢查一下。
heal　v. 治療：A physician's duty is to heal the sick. 醫生的責任是治病救人。
treat　v. 治療，醫治：Are they able to treat this disease?他們能夠治療這種病嗎？

【參考答案】

　　1. (D)　　　　2. (A)　　　　3. (F)　　　　4. (C)　　　　5. (B)

Unit 34

題材　周圍的人　　詞數　190　　建議閱讀時間　4.5 分鐘

A man went to a fast-food restaurant to buy his lunch. "Hi," a worker said. "May I help you?" "I'd like a hamburger, large chips, and a Coke," the man said.

"Anything else?" the worker asked. "No," the man answered. "That's it."

"Is that for here or to go?" the worker asked. "To go," the man said.

The worker put the man's lunch in a bag. The man took out his money and paid for his lunch. "Thank you," the worker said. "Have a nice day."

The man took the bag and walked to a park. He sat down and opened the bag. He was surprised. There was no hamburger in the bag. There were no chips. There was no Coke. There was only money in the bag—a lot of money! The man counted the money. Two thousand dollars! Why was the money in the bag? Where was the man's lunch?

The manager of the fast-food restaurant needed to go to the bank. He put two thousand dollars in an envelope. He put the envelope in a bag and put the bag down. The worker gave the manager's bag to the man by mistake. So the manager had a hamburger, chips and a Coke, and the man had two thousand dollars. What should the man do?

---
envelope：信封

閱讀上面的短文，選擇正確答案。

(　　) 1. The man went to a restaurant to _____.
A. buy his lunch B. have a rest　C. cook food　　D. sell drinks

(　　) 2. The man wanted to have his lunch _____.
A. in a hotel　　　　　　　B. in a restaurant
C. in a shop　　　　　　　D. in a park

(　　) 3. When the man opened the bag, he found _____ in it.
A. food　　　　B. drink　　　　C. money　　　　D. nothing

(　　) 4. _____ couldn't find his money.
A. The man　　B. The manager C. The worker　D. Nobody

◀參考譯文▶

　　一位男士去快餐店買午餐。「您好，」一位服務員說，「您需要什麼？」「我買一個漢堡，大份薯片和一杯可樂，」這位男士說。

　　「還需要別的嗎？」服務員問。「不需要了，」這位男士回答道。「就這些。」

　　「在這裡吃還是帶走？」服務員問。「帶走，」男士回答說。

　　服務員把男士的午餐裝進袋子。這名男士掏錢付賬。「謝謝，」服務員說。「祝您愉快。」

　　這位男士拿著袋子走向公園。他坐下來打開袋子。他吃了一驚。裏面沒有漢堡，也沒有薯片，也沒有可樂。袋子裏只有錢——很多的錢！這位男士數了數，有 2,000 美元！袋子裏怎麼會有錢呢？這位男士的午餐哪去了？

　　原來是這麼回事：快餐店的經理要去銀行。他把 2,000 美元放進了一隻信封。再把信封放進袋子，擱在一邊。服務員弄錯了，他把給經理的袋子給了這位男士。這樣，經理拿到了漢堡、薯片和可樂，而這位男士有了 2,000 美元。這位男士該怎麼辦呢？

---

fast-food　adj. 供應快餐的，快餐式的：a fast-food restaurant 快餐店

count　v. 數，清點：We counted the people present， there were 20. 我們清點了出席的人數，總共 20 個。

envelope　n. 信封：After writing a letter， you address the envelope, seal it and stick a stamp in the top right-hand corner. 寫好了信，就在信封上寫上地址，把信封封口，把郵票貼在信封的右上角。

by mistake　錯誤地：I used your towel by mistake. 我錯用了你的毛巾。

◀參考答案▶

　　1. (A)　　　　2. (D)　　　　3. (C)　　　　4. (B)

Unit 35

題材 歷史和地理　　**詞數** 156　　**建議閱讀時間** 4.5分鐘

The people of Mexico also built pyramids. They didn't build them for tombs. They built a pyramid and then built a temple on top of it. The pyramids of Mexico are not as high as the pyramids of Egypt, but they are big. Inside the pyramids there is nothing, only dirt and stones.

The biggest pyramid in Mexico is almost 2,000 years old. Scientists think it took 10,000 men more than ten years to build it. On the top they built a temple to the sun. The temple is no longer there, but people called it the Pyramid of the Sun. Near it is another huge pyramid, the Pyramid of the Moon.

How were the people of Mexico able to build the pyramids thousands of years ago? How did they carry and lift the huge stones? Each stone fit so well and they didn't have our modern machines!

The pyramids of Egypt and Mexico have been studied by many people, but nobody can say just how they were built.

Mexico：墨西哥　pyramid：金字塔　tomb：墳墓　Egypt：埃及　dirt：泥土、髒物

閱讀上面的短文，選擇正確答案。

(　　) 1. On top of the pyramids of Mexico there _____.
A. were tombs　　　　　　B. were temples
C. were mummies　　　　D. was nothing

(　　) 2. The pyramids of Mexico are _____ the pyramids of Egypt.
A. higher than　B. lower than　C. as high as　D. as low as

(　　) 3. There _____ inside the pyramids in Mexico.
A. are dead bodies　　　B. are treasures
C. is only dirt and stones　D. are temples

(　　) 4. On top of the Pyramid of the Sun _____.
A. there was once a temple
B. there is still a temple
C. there is a tomb
D. there were the bodies of the king and the queen

(　　) 5. ＿＿＿＿ how the people of Mexico built their pyramids.

      A. Everybody knows   B. Many scientists can say

      C. Everyone of us can say   D. No one knows

【參考譯文】

　　墨西哥人也建造了金字塔。他們建造金字塔不是作墳墓用的。他們每建造一座金字塔就要在上面建一座神廟。墨西哥的金字塔沒有埃及金字塔那麼高，但它們很大。金字塔內部什麼東西都沒有，只有沙土和石頭。

　　墨西哥最大的金字塔距今已有近兩千年。科學家認為，一萬人花了十多年的時間才建成它。在金字塔的頂部，他們建了一座太陽神廟。廟已經不復存在，但人們還把它叫做太陽金字塔。在它附近，還有一座巨大的金字塔，它叫做月亮金字塔。

　　數千年前，墨西哥人是怎樣建成這些金字塔的呢？他們怎樣搬運並抬起這些巨石？每塊石頭契合得如此之好，而他們並沒有現代化的工具！

　　許多人對埃及金字塔和墨西哥金字塔做了大量研究，但沒有人能搞清楚它們到底是怎樣建成的。

---

tomb　n. 墳墓：He was buried in the family tomb. 他被葬於家族的墳墓中。

temple　n. 神殿，廟宇：Greek temples were beautifully built. 希臘的神殿都建得很漂亮。

dirt　n. 髒東西；泥土：Wash the dirt off the kitchen floor. 把廚房地上的污垢沖洗乾淨。

  ‖**dirty**　adj. 骯髒的

【參考答案】

    1. (B)   2. (B)   3. (C)   4. (A)   5. (D)

Unit 36

題材 應對考試	詞數 162	建議閱讀時間 4分鐘

Many people find exams a frightening experience. Sitting down for an exam when everybody is so quiet and serious makes most people nervous.

But there are a few things you can do to relax before you start. At the beginning of an exam, read all the instructions carefully so you know exactly ___1___. Work out how much time you can spend on each question. If you feel yourself getting nervous at any time, stop what you are doing and take a few deep breaths.

However, the most useful things are always done before you get to the exam room. You may do some practice tests and ___2___ in a right way. And then the real thing will seem much easier.

You also need to remember that exams are not the most important things in the world — even though you fail, you can do better next time. The more you take, ___3___.

---

relax：放鬆　　instruction：指導；指示　　exactly：確定的

閱讀上面的短文，選擇正確答案。

(　　) 1.　A. what you have to do
　　　　　　C. how to do next step

　　　　　　B. the time you can use
　　　　　　D. how to review

(　　) 2.　A. take a rest
　　　　　　C. review your lessons

　　　　　　B. close your books
　　　　　　D. check the notes

(　　) 3.　A. the more worried you will be
　　　　　　B. the less worried you will be
　　　　　　C. the more knowledge you can get
　　　　　　D. the less knowledge you can get

◀參考譯文▶

許多人覺得考試是一件很嚇人的事情。每個人都安安靜靜、嚴肅認真地坐在那兒，這樣的場景讓大多數人都感到緊張。

為了讓自己放鬆，考前你還是能做點事情的。考試開始的時候，仔細閱讀所有的說明，這樣你就能準確地知道你必須做什麼。確定每道題應該用多少時間。假如你覺得自己一直很緊張，停下正在做的事，深呼吸幾次。

　　然而，最有用的措施還是在進考場前做好準備。你可以做一些測驗卷，以此復習自己的功課，這是一種正確的方法。到了真正上考場的時候，考試似乎就變得容易多了。

　　你還應該明白，考試並不是世界上最重要的事情——即使你不及格，下次你也能考好。你參加考試的次數越多，你就越不會擔心。

---

instruction　n. 指示，說明：Read the instructions on the back of the packet carefully. 包裝背面有使用說明，請仔細閱讀。

work out 計劃，決定，制訂出：I've drawn up the main outlines, and we'll work out the details later. 我已擬訂出總提綱，下面我們把細節制訂出來。

practice　n. 實習，演習；練習：The young teachers are now doing their teaching practice. 青年教師正在搞教學實習。

the real thing 真跡，原作：This painting is just a copy. The real thing is in a gallery. 這幅畫只是複製品，原作藏於美術館內。

【參考答案】

Thursday

1. (A)　　　　2. (C)　　　　3. (B)

Unit 37

| 題材 | 朋友和周圍的人 | 詞數 | 196 | 建議閱讀時間 | 5 分鐘 |

▶Hilda Conkling was just four years old when she made up her first poems. Since Hilda could not write, her mother wrote down Hilda's words.

When Hilda was eight years old, her mother sent the poems to magazines. The poems were printed in 2013. When Hilda turned ten, her first book, Poems by a Little Girl, was published. Everyone who read the book was amazed. "I know of no other example in which such really beautiful poetry has been written by a child," one reader said.

Hilda's book was then entered in a contest. The works of more than one hundred other poets, all grownups, were in the contest. Hilda's book won the contest.

▶When Kim was four years old, her parents gave her a set of paints. Kim loved the present and began painting pictures every day. Soon she was painting beautiful pictures of trees, houses, mountains, and even people. Kim entered school a year later, but she didn't stop painting. By the time she was in the third grade, she had painted two hundred pictures.

Then Kim decided to have an art show. Her mother baked cookies and served lemonade. Kim hung her pictures all around the house. All of Kim's friends came to her art show. They enjoyed looking at her paintings. They also enjoyed eating the cookies and sipping the lemonade.

> publish：出版　amaze：驚訝　contest：競賽　grownup：成人　lemonade：檸檬汁
> sipping：啜飲

閱讀上面的短文，選擇正確答案。

(　) 1.　Hilda began making up poems when she was _____.
　　　　A. ten years old　　　　　　B. eight years old
　　　　C. an adult　　　　　　　　D. four years old

(　) 2.　Hilda's poems were first published in _____.
　　　　A. letters　　　B. a book　　　C. magazines　　　D. newspapers

（　　）3.　You can tell that Hilda Conkling _____.
　　　A. loved poetry　　　　　　　　B. loved the outdoors
　　　C. had no friends　　　　　　　D. did not go to school

（　　）4.　The story says that Kim painted pictures of _____.
　　　A. animals　　　B. lakes　　　　C. mountains　　　D. schools

（　　）5.　At the show, Kim's mother served _____.
　　　A. hot dogs　　　B. soup　　　　C. milk　　　　D. lemonade

（　　）6.　You can tell that Kim _____.
　　　A. liked watching TV　　　　　B. liked to paint
　　　C. could bake cookies　　　　　D. had no friends

【參考譯文】

▶ 西爾達·康克琳年僅四歲就創作了自己的第一首詩。由於她還不會寫字，媽媽替她記下了所說的話。

西爾達八歲時，媽媽把她寫的詩寄給多家雜誌。2013 年，她的詩作發表了。十歲時，她的第一本書《小女孩的詩》出版了。讀到這本書的人都很驚訝。「我不知道還有哪本書是出自孩子之手、詩句還能如此美妙的，」一位讀者說。

後來，西爾達的書參加了一次評選。參賽的還有一百多位其他詩人的作品，他們全是成年人。西爾達的書獲了獎。

▶金四歲時，父母給她買了一套塗料，她非常喜歡這個禮物，每天都用它來畫畫。很快，她就能畫各式各樣漂亮的圖案了，有樹木、房屋、山川，甚至人物。一年後，金上學了，但她並沒有停止畫畫。三年級時，金已經畫了兩百幅畫。

這時，金決定辦一次畫展，媽媽負責給客人烘制餅乾、端檸檬汁。金將畫作掛滿整幢房子，她所有的朋友都來觀看，朋友們非常喜歡這些畫作，也喜歡金媽媽準備的餅乾和檸檬汁。

poetry　n. 詩，詩歌：This dancer has poetry in her movements. 這位女舞蹈演員的動作富有詩意。

contest　n. 競賽，比賽：Who will judge the speech contest? 誰擔任演講比賽的裁判？

sip　v. 小口地喝，抿：She was already sitting at the bar, sipping wine. 她已經坐在酒吧裏，小口地喝酒。

【參考答案】

1. (D)　　　2. (C)　　　3. (A)　　　4. (C)　　　5. (D)
6. (B)

Unit 38

題材　朋友和周圍的人　　詞數　206　　建議閱讀時間　5 分鐘

There is a bar in our town with the name "The White Horse". It is Mr. Webster's. Few people went to the bar last year, but things are quite different now.

There was a picture of a white horse on the door of the bar. Then a stranger came in one day, drank something, looked around the bar, and then said to Mr. Webster, "Few people come here. Take down the picture of the white horse and put a picture of a black horse instead."

"But the name of the bar is 'The White Horse'." Mr. Webster said.

"Yes, but do it," the man said. Then he went out of the bar.

Mr. Webster went to an artist and said, "I want a picture of a black horse."

The next day a picture of a black horse was on the door of the bar instead of that of the white horse. Soon after the door opened, a man came in and said, "There's a mistake on the door of your bar, and the picture is different from the name." The man looked, sat down and drank something.

Then another man came in and said the same, and then another and another. A lot of people came in and said, "The picture on your door is wrong," and they all stopped and drank in Mr. Webster's bar.

---

bar：酒吧　instead：而不是

閱讀上面的短文，選擇正確答案。

(　　) 1. The stranger told Mr. Webster to take down the picture of the white horse because he knew _____.

A. a picture of a black horse showed good luck

B. the picture of the white horse wasn't good for the bar

C. people would come in and tell the picture was different from the name

D. people would understand the picture different from the name

(　　) 2.　Mr. Webster agreed with the stranger _____.

　　A. though he wasn't ready to do it at first

　　B. because he knew he was an artist

　　C. though he didn't like the black horse

　　D. because he also wanted to change the picture

(　　) 3.　More and more people came to the bar because _____.

　　A. it had changed its name

　　B. the black horse was better than the white one

　　C. the bar had a black horse

　　D. they wanted to show the mistake

(　　) 4.　The stranger _____.

　　A. was cleverer than Mr. Webster

　　B. didn't like the white horse at the beginning

　　C. knew Mr. Webster and the artist

　　D. got much money by teaching Mr.Webster

(　　) 5.　From the story we have learnt that _____.

　　A. if your business is not good, you'd better change the name or the picture

　　B. if you are in trouble, you should take others' ideas

　　C. when you have difficulty, don't give up

　　D. when a good name is given, it can cause success

◀參考譯文▶

　　我們鎮子上有一家叫做「白馬」的酒吧。他是韋伯斯特先生開的。去年很少有人光顧這裏，但現在的情形不同了。

　　酒吧的門上畫有一匹白馬。有一天，一位陌生人走了進來，他喝了點兒東西，四處看看，然後對韋伯斯特先生說：「很少有人光顧這裏。把白馬的畫摘下來，換一幅黑馬吧。」

　　「但酒吧的名字是『白馬』呀，」韋伯斯特先生說。

　　「是這樣，但照我說的去做吧，」這位男人說完就走了。

　　韋伯斯特先生找到一名藝術家，並對他說，「我想要一幅黑馬的畫作。」

　　第二天，一幅黑馬代替白馬貼在了酒吧的門上。開始營業不一會兒，一位男人走了進來，他說：「你們酒吧的門上有一處錯誤，畫和名字不相符。」這位男人看了看，坐下來喝了點東西。

　　後來，又一位男人走了進來，也說了同樣的話，這樣的人接踵而來。他們都進來說：「你們門上的畫錯了。」他們都在韋伯斯特先生的酒吧停下來喝了些東西。

---

bar　n. 酒吧：They had a drink in the bar before the meal. 他們吃飯前在酒吧喝了一杯酒。

stranger　n. 陌生人；外地人，新來者：Don't get into cars with strangers. 別坐陌生人的車。

instead of　代替，而不是：They went there on foot instead of by bus. 他們沒乘公共汽車而是步行到那裏去的。

◖**參考答案**◗

1. (C)　　　　2. (A)　　　　3. (D)　　　　4. (A)　　　　5. (B)

Unit 39

題材　學校生活　　　詞數　266　　　建議閱讀時間　6.5分鐘

My class will put on a short play in English at the end of the year. Yesterday our English teacher gave us copies of the play.

"Choose a character in the play that you'd like to be," she told us. "This afternoon learn a few lines of this part for homework. Then tomorrow you can say those lines in front of the class. I'll decide who play each part."

I wanted to have one of the bigger parts in the play, so I choose the part of the king. He has a lot of lines to say. I learned them by heart.

This morning in our English lesson we had to say our lines. I acted the part of the king. When I said my lines, I put a lot of expression into my acting. I thought I acted really well.

Everyone in the class read a part and then the teacher decided who would play each part.

Many of the students in my class couldn't act at all. They couldn't even read without making lots of mistakes. I was sure that I would get a big part in the play.

However, the teacher gave me the part of a soldier. He has only one line. It is, "Yes, sir!"

I was very disappointed. At the end of the lesson I went up to her and asked her why I had such a small part.

"You put too much <u>expression</u> in your acting," she said. "Good acting is not big acting. It is acting the audience can believe in."

I think I know what she means.

---

expression：表情　　disappointed：失望　　audience：觀眾、聽眾

閱讀上面的短文，選擇正確答案。

(　　) 1.　What did the boy want to do in the play?

　　　　　A. To get an important part.　　B. To organize the play.

　　　　　C. To work the lights.　　　　D. To get a large acting part.

(　　) 2. How did the boy feel when the teacher told the class they would put on a play?

    A. Bored.   B. Excited.   C. Sad   D. Unhappy.

(　　) 3. Why didn't the teacher give him the part of the king?

    A. He did not act correctly.   B. He did not know the lines.

    C. He was not handsome.   D. He was too short.

(　　) 4. What does the underlined word "expression" in the passage mean?

    A. 表情   B. 建議   C. 模仿   D. 服飾

【參考譯文】

年末我們班將用英語表演一個短劇。昨天，英語老師把表演的劇本給了我們。

「選一個你想飾演的劇中角色，」她告訴我們。「今天下午，你們的作業就是記幾句所選角色的臺詞。明天，你們要在全班同學面前說那些臺詞。我再決定誰演哪個角色。」

我想成爲劇中戲份較重的角色，因此選擇了國王。他有很多臺詞要說。我把臺詞全都背了下來。

今天早上的英語課，我們得說臺詞了。我扮演國王。說臺詞時，我在表演中加入了豐富的表情。我以爲自己演得很棒。

班裏的每個人都說了一個角色的臺詞，然後老師決定誰來扮演哪個角色。

班裏的很多學生根本不會表演，甚至不能在不犯很多錯誤的情況下念完臺詞。所以我很確信自己將在劇中扮演重要角色。

然而，老師卻給我了一個士兵的角色。他只有一句臺詞，就是：「是的，先生！」

我非常失望。下課時，我走到老師跟前，問她爲什麼讓我表演這麼一個小角色。

「你在表演中加入了太多的表情，」她說。「好的表演不是誇張的表演，而是讓觀衆信以爲眞的表演。」

我想我明白了她的意思。

---

line n. 臺詞：In the last act, I had four lines. 在最後一幕，我有四句臺詞。

part n. 角色：He played the part of Hamlet. 他飾演哈姆雷特。

【參考答案】

1. (D)   2. (B)   3. (A)   4. (A)

Unit 40

| 題材 | 作家生平 | 詞數 | 177 | 建議閱讀時間 | 4.5 分鐘 |

Guy De Maupassant was born in Normandy in France in 1850. His parents separated when he was about six, and he went to live with his mother. At the age of thirteen, he was __1__ to school. There he was praised for a(n) __2__ poem he wrote. In this way he began his writing at a(n) __3__ age. During the Franco-Prussian War, he had to __4__ writing. After the war, he went to Paris to look for a job which he hoped that would __5__ him free time to write. It was in Paris that he met great writers, from whom he __6__ a great deal.

__7__ he found material for many stories while working as a clerk, he found life in the office restricted. After one of his stories was published, he left his office in order to spend __8__ time in writing. At the age of thirty-four, he became quite __9__. During this time, he wrote some of his best-known works __10__ The Necklace, one of the most famous short stories in the world.

---

separated：分居、離異　material：材料　restricted：受限制的

閱讀上面的短文，選擇正確答案。

(　) 1.　A. sent　　　B.asked　　　C.told　　　D.found

(　) 2.　A. simple　　B.bad　　　　C.excellent　D.active

(　) 3.　A. first　　　B.last　　　　C.late　　　　D.early

(　) 4.　A. grow up　B.catch up　　C.give up　　D.hurry up

(　) 5.　A. begin　　　B.leave　　　C.open　　　D.turn

(　) 6.　A. worked　　B.studied　　C.learned　　D.lived

(　) 7.　A. When　　　B.Before　　C.If　　　　　D.Though

(　) 8.　A. empty　　　B.full　　　　C.free　　　　D.extra

(　) 9.　A. bright　　　B.healthy　　C.famous　　D.lucky

(　) 10. A. meaning　　B.including　C.taking　　D.speaking

【參考譯文】

　　蓋伊·德·莫泊桑於 1850 年生於法國的諾曼底。6 歲時，他的父母離異了，他跟母親一起生活。13 歲時，他開始上學。在學校，因爲他寫了一首優美的詩歌而受到讚揚，他就這樣開始了早期的寫作生涯。普法戰爭期間，他不得不放棄寫作。戰爭結束後，他來到巴黎，希望找一份空閒時間能寫作的工作。在那裏，他遇到了一些偉大的作家，並因此而受益匪淺。

　　儘管在做職員期間他積累了很多故事素材，但他發現辦公室的工作限制了他的創作。於是，當他的一篇小説發表後，他便辭去工作，專心從事寫作。34 歲時，他已非常有名了。在此期間，他創作出一些最著名的作品，其中包括《項鏈》，這是世界上最著名的短篇小説之一。

---

separate v. 分居，疏遠：Her parents separated when she was eleven. 她 11 歲時，父母離異了。

Franco- 用於構成複合詞，表示"法國（人）的，法國（人）和……的"

restrict v. 限制，約束：He feels this new law will restrict his freedom. 他覺得這條新法律將會限制他的自由。‖**restricted** adj. 受限制的，被限定的

【參考答案】

1. (A)	2. (C)	3. (D)	4. (C)	5. (B)
6. (C)	7. (D)	8. (B)	9. (C)	10. (B)

Unit 41

題材　熱點話題　　　詞數　114　　　建議閱讀時間　3 分鐘

Families in Canada have changed in the last 50 years.

In the 1950, most families had two parents. The father went to work and the mother stayed home with two or more children. How are the families different in the 2000s?

Families are smaller　The average family has 3.1 people.

Single-parent families　One out of five children lives in a single-parent family. Most single parents are women.

Common-law families　One out of ten children is raised by parents who are not legally married to each other.

Working mothers　More mothers work outside the home. Sixty-four percent of married women with children under 16 work outside the home.

Divorce and remarriage　Forty-one percent of all marriages end in divorce. Thirty percent of all marriages are remarriages.

---
average：平均的　Common-law families：非婚姻家庭　legally：合法的　divorce：離婚
remarriage：再婚　marriage：婚姻

閱讀上面的短文，選擇正確答案。

（　　）1.　Less than of all marriage are remarriages.
　　　　A. one-four　　　B. one-third　　　C. one-sixth　　　D. one-fifth

（　　）2.　From this passage we can infer that _____.
　　　　A. the families in the 2000s have fewer people than those in the 1950s
　　　　B. 64% of women are married when they are under 16
　　　　C. 59% of all marriages end in divorce
　　　　D. one-fifth of the children are raised by their fathers when their parents get divorced

(　) 3. Compared with 1950s, more mothers in the 2000s _____.

　　A. go out to work in order to make a living

　　B. raise their children when they get divorced

　　C. stay at home to look after their children and do housework

　　D. A and B

【參考譯文】

　　在過去的 50 年裏，加拿大的家庭已經發生了許多變化。

　　在 20 世紀 50 年代，大多數家庭父母雙全。父親去工作，母親待在家裏照顧兩個或更多的孩子。而 21 世紀的家庭情況有什麼不同呢？

　　家庭更小　平均每個家庭有 3.1 個人。

　　單親家庭　每 5 個孩子就有一個生活在單親家庭裏。大多數單親家長是婦女。

　　非正式婚姻家庭　每 10 個孩子中就有一個是由非正式結婚的父母撫養的。

　　母親工作　更多的母親外出工作。孩子年齡在 16 歲以下的已婚婦女中，有 64%外出工作。

　　離婚和再婚　在所有的婚姻中，41%的婚姻以離婚收場，30%的婚姻屬於再婚。

---

average　adj.　平均的：What is the average rainfall for April?四月份的平均雨量是多少？

single　adj.　單獨的，單個的：a single track 單軌 ‖ **single-parent**　adj.　單親的

common　adj.　普通的：common salt 食鹽 ‖ **common-law**　adj.　普通法的：common-law marriage 非正式婚姻

legally　adv.　合法地：They are not legally married. 他們沒有正式結婚。

divorce　n.　離婚：She obtained a divorce after years of unhappiness. 多年的痛苦之後，她終於離婚了。

remarriage　n.　再婚

【參考答案】

　　1. (B)　　　　　2. (A)　　　　　3. (D)

Unit 42

題材　學校生活　　　詞數　167　　　建議閱讀時間　4 分鐘

There would be a school party on Friday evening. The girls were talking excitedly. "I'm going to wear a black dress, so everybody will notice me," said Emily. "How about you, Linda?" "I'm not sure. Maybe jeans, an old shirt, and a hat. People will notice me more than you!" Linda said.

"What are we going to do about the boys?" asked Jane. "Do you remember the last school party? They just stood there, and we girls had to dance by ourselves!" said Joan. "I hear that some of the boys learned how to dance this summer. Maybe it'll be better this time," said Mary.

The party was held on Friday evening. Groups of students arrived. The music began. The girls stood in a line on one side, and the boys on another side. Mr.　Green, their teacher, tried to get them together, but failed.

After a while Tim said, "I don't want to stand here the whole time. The party is only for two hours. It'll be over soon." He started to dance. All the others watched him. Then David asked Emily if she wanted to dance. Then Jack and Linda. Then, all began to dance. Soon there were more dancers than watchers.

閱讀上面的短文，回答問題。

(　　) 1.　What were the girls talking about?
　　　　A. The dress and the boys.　　　B. The teacher and the boys.
　　　　C. The food and the dress.　　　D. The jeans and the hat.

(　　) 2.　What happened when the music began?
　　　　A. The girls and the boys began to dance.
　　　　B. The girls and the boys stood together.
　　　　C. The girls stood in front of the boys.
　　　　D. The girls stood on one side, and the boys on another side.

(　　) 3.　When did the boy learn to dance?
　　　　A. This summer.　　　　　　　B. Last winter.
　　　　C. Last party.　　　　　　　　D. This speing.

(　　) 4.　How long did the party last?

      A. One hour.　　　　　　　　　B. Two hours.

      C. Three hours.　　　　　　　　D. One and Half hours.

(　　) 5.　Who was the first one to dance?

      A. David.　　　B. Tim.　　　C. Emily　　　D. Jack.

◖參考譯文◗

　　週五晚上，學校要舉辦舞會。女孩們興奮地談論著。「我要穿一襲黑裙，這樣，每個人都會注意到我，」埃米莉說。「你怎麼樣，琳達？」「我還拿不定主意。也許是一條牛仔褲再加一件舊襯衫，外帶一頂帽子。人們會更關注我而不是你。」琳達說。

　　「對那些男孩該怎麼辦？」簡說。「你還記得上一次學校舉辦舞會的情形嗎？他們只會站在那兒，我們女孩只好自己跳！」瓊說。「我聽說今年夏天有些男孩學會了跳舞。也許這次會好些，」瑪麗說。

　　舞會在週五晚上舉行。成群結隊的學生來到這裏。音樂響起來了。女孩們在一邊排成一排，男孩們在另一邊。他們的老師格林先生想把他們撮合到一塊，但沒成功。

　　過了一會兒，蒂姆說：「我不想一直站在這兒。舞會只有兩個小時，很快就會結束的。」他開始跳舞。其他人在旁邊看。這時，戴維邀請埃米莉共舞。接著又是傑克和琳達。再後來，所有的人都跳了起來。很快，跳舞的人就比站在一旁看的人多了。

---

excitedly adv.　激動地，興奮地：We're all talking excitedly at the thought of moving into our new house. 一想到要搬進新房子，我們都興奮地聊起來。

jean n.　（常作 jeans）牛仔褲：These jeans are a bit too tight. 這條牛仔褲緊了點兒。

◖參考答案◗

  1. (A)　　　　2. (D)　　　　3. (A)　　　　4. (B)　　　　5. (B)

Unit 43

題材 學校生活　　**詞數** 194　　**建議閱讀時間** 5 分鐘

Several days ago, some students from the US visited our school. When we talked, I discovered __1__ differences in school life between the US and Taiwan. For example, each class __2__ fifty minutes in the US. It is a little __3__ than that in Taiwan. We usually have forty or forty-five minutes in each class. Another difference is that they have less break time between __4__. Besides, although most schools in both countries finish their __5__ classes at 12 o'clock, the students in the US only have an hour-long break, so they __6__ eat lunch quickly. Their afternoon classes begin at 1:00 p.m. and school is over __7__ 3:00 p.m. Then they take part in club activities or play sports.

Many Taiwanese students don't work during their high school years, while the US students like to find a part-time job in __8__ free time. They don't have a dream job in mind. They think __9__ is no difference between jobs. Working is a useful experience for them and they can make money at the same time. Some of them even take one-year full-time jobs __10__ they leave high school and then go to college.

> **break**　n.（課間）休息：The coach told us to take a break for five minutes. 教練讓我們休息 5 分鐘。

閱讀上面的短文，選擇正確答案。

(　) 1.　A. no　　　　B.few　　　　C.little　　　　D.some
(　) 2.　A. lasts　　　B.finishes　　C.starts　　　D.stays
(　) 3.　A. shorter　　B.longer　　　C.earlier　　　D.later
(　) 4.　A. schools　　B.classes　　　C.meals　　　D.students
(　) 5.　A. day　　　　B.night　　　　C.morning　　D.afternoon
(　) 6.　A. can't　　　B.mustn't　　　C.need to　　　D.are able to
(　) 7.　A. in　　　　B.for　　　　　C.during　　　D.around
(　) 8.　A. my　　　　B.his　　　　　C.their　　　　D.your
(　) 9.　A. it　　　　B.there　　　　C.that　　　　D.this
(　) 10.　A. after　　　B.with　　　　C.while　　　　D.during

◖參考譯文◗

　　前幾天，一些美國學生訪問了我們學校。交談過程中，我發現美國和台灣的學校生活之間存在一些差異。比如，美國一節課是 50 分鐘，比台灣略長，我們一般是一節課 40 或 45 分鐘。另一個差異是美國的課間休息時間我們短。此外，儘管兩國的大多數學校都在 12 點結束上午的課程，但美國學生僅有一小時的中午休息時間，所以他們必須儘快吃完午餐。他們下午的課程從 1 點開始，3 點左右放學。然後，他們就可以參加俱樂部活動或體育活動了。

　　許多台灣學生在讀高中期間不會去工作，而美國學生喜歡在業餘時間打打零工。在他們的觀念裏，沒有什麼理想的工作之說，他們認為各種工作之間沒有差別。工作對他們來說只是一種有益的體驗，同時還能掙到錢。他們中的一些人高中畢業後甚至會從事一年的全職工作，然後再去上大學。

◖參考答案◗

1. (D)	2. (A)	3. (B)	4. (B)	5. (C)
6. (C)	7. (D)	8. (C)	9. (B)	10. (A)

Unit 44

題材　科學與技術　　　詞數　166　　　建議閱讀時間　4分鐘

Today people can use the phone to talk with others almost anywhere on the earth. But when you use the phone, you don't see the person you are talking with. That may change in the near future.

Today some people are using a kind of telephone called the picture phone or vision phone. With it, two people who are talking can see each other.

Picture phones can be useful when you have something to show the person you're calling. They may have other uses in the future. One day you may be able to ring up a library and ask to see a book.

Then you'll be able to read the book right over your picture phone. Or you may be able to go shopping through your picture phone. If you see something in the newspaper that you think you want to buy, you'll go to your phone and call the shop. People at the shop will show you the thing through the phone. You'll be able to shop all over town and never even leave your room!

---

vision：視覺；影像

閱讀上面的短文，選擇正確答案。

(　　) 1.　Today people can use the phone to talk with others _____.
　　　　A. in all the towns
　　　　B. in some places in the world
　　　　C. almost anywhere on the earth
　　　　D. only in big cities

(　　) 2.　The word "it" in the text means _____.
　　　　A. the picture phone　　　　B. the use
　　　　C. any phone　　　　　　　D. the change

(　　) 3.　We can _____ through the picture phone according to the text.
　　　　A. write a book　　　　　　B. do shopping
　　　　C. play games　　　　　　　D. have classes

(　　) 4.　What are the shortcomings of today's phone?

A. You can't hear clearly on the phone.

B. You can't use it to ring up a library.

C. You can't talk with two persons at the same time.

D. You can't see the person you are talking with.

〔參考譯文〕

現在，人們可以通過電話和地球上幾乎任何地方的人交談。但使用電話時，你看不到通話的對象。這種狀況可能在不久的將來發生改變。

現在，有些人在使用一種影像電話。有了它，兩個人在通話的同時還能看到對方。

當你有某樣東西要展示給你正在通話的人看時，影像電話就派上了用場。將來，它們可能還會具備其他功能。某一天，你可能給圖書館打電話，請他們幫你尋找一本書。

這時，你完全可以通過影像電話讀這本書。你還可以通過影像電話購物。假如你在報紙上看到了某樣東西，而且你想買，你就可以來到電話機旁，撥商店的號碼。商店的工作人員通過電話給你看這樣東西。你甚至不出家門就可以在整個小城購物了。

---

vision n. 視力，視覺；圖像：We apologize for temporary loss of TV vision. 我們對電視影像一度消失表示歉意。

shop n. 商店，店鋪 v. 到商店去購物：go shopping 去買東西

according to 根據：According to my watch it is four o'clock. 根據我的表，現在是四點鐘。

shortcoming n. 短處：You've got to realize your own shortcomings. 你必須認識自己的缺點。

〔參考答案〕

1. (C)　　　　2. (A)　　　　3. (B)　　　　4. (D)

Unit 45

題材　社會　　　詞數　192　　　建議閱讀時間　5分鐘

A man once had a dream about the Black Forest in Germany. In his dream he was walking in the forest when two men ran out and tried to throw him to the ground. He ran off as fast as he could, but they followed him. He reached a place where he saw two roads in front of him, one to the right and the other to the left. Which road should he take?

He heard the two men behind him, getting nearer, and at the same time he heard a voice in his ear. It told him to go to the right, and he did so. He ran on and soon came to a small hotel. He was received there kindly and given a room, and he was saved from the two men. That was the dream.

Twenty years later he was really in the Black Forest and, as happened in the dream long ago, two men ran out and tried to throw him down. He ran off, and came to a place with two roads, like in the dream. He remembered the dream and took the road to the right. He soon reached a small hotel, was taken in, and so was safe. His dream of twenty years before had saved his life.

閱讀上面的短文，選擇正確答案。

(　) 1.　The Black Forest is _____.
　　　　A. a place in Germany　　　　B. not a real place
　　　　C. a place in Britain　　　　D. invented by the writer

(　) 2.　When he was walking in the forest, _____ ran after him.
　　　　A. two dogs　　B. two tigers　　C. two women　　D. two men

(　) 3.　Finally he came to _____.
　　　　A. a forest　　　　　　　　B. another road
　　　　C. another dream　　　　　　D. a small hotel

(　) 4.　It was _____ that saved the man's life 20 years later.
　　　　A. a voice　　　　　　　　B. the dream
　　　　C. someone else　　　　　　D. God

(　　) 5.　The story tells us that _____.

A. a dream may come true some time later

B. a dream is always a dream

C. people should not believe their dreams

D. people should always believe their dreams

【參考譯文】

　　一名男士曾經做過有關德國黑森林（位於德國西南部的巴登符騰堡州)的夢。在夢中，他行走在森林裏，這時有兩個人跑出來，想把他摔倒在地。他竭盡全力地飛跑，但他們一直跟著。他來到一個地方，面前有兩條路，一條通往右邊，一條通往左邊。他該走哪條路呢？

　　他聽見身後的兩個人已越跑越近，同時他也聽見耳朵裏有説話的聲音。聲音告訴他往右走，他就照做了。他跑啊跑，很快來到一間小旅館。那裏的人熱情地接待了他，並給他安排了一個房間，他躲過了那兩個人。這就是他的夢。

　　20 年後，他真的來到了黑森林，正如許多年前夢中的情節一樣，兩個人跑了出來，想把他摔倒。他立刻逃跑，來到了一處和夢裏一樣的岔路口。他還記得那個夢，於是往右跑。他很快來到一間小旅館，並被安排下住宿，這樣他就安全了。20 年前的夢救了他的命。

---

throw v.　扔，投；使倒下，摔倒：throw sB. to the ground 把某人摔倒在地/The bus braked and we were thrown to the floor. 公共汽車突然刹車，我們都跌倒了。

take in　接待，留宿；接受，收容：The hotels were full, but some kind friends took us in for the night. 所有的旅館都客滿了，但一些善良的朋友接待我們在家中過夜。

invent v.　發明；編造：They invented an excuse for having to leave earlier than usual. 他們為提前離開編造了一個藉口。

come true（希望、理想等）變成現實：One's dreams do not always come true. 一個人的夢想並不一定能變成現實。

【參考答案】

1. (A)　　　　2. (C)　　　　3. (D)　　　　4. (B)　　　　5. (A)

Unit 46

題材　獨佔與分享　　詞數　188　　建議閱讀時間　4.5 分鐘

A rich farmer in England once had a friend who grew very good apples. One day this friend gave the farmer a fine young tree and told him to take it home and plant it. The farmer was __1__ with the present but when he came home he did not know __2__ to plant the tree. He thought, "If I plant it near the road, __3__ will steal the apples. If I plant it in my field, my neighbors will come at night and rob me. If I plant it near my house, my children will take the apples."

At last he planted the tree __4__ in a wood where __5__ could see it. But the tree could not grow without __6__ and died. When the farmer's friend __7__ of it he got very angry and asked the farmer why he had planted the tree in such a __8__ place. "Where could I plant it?" the farmer said, and told the friend his anxiety.

"But then somebody would have __9__ the apples," said his friend, "and now nobody can have them and you have __10__ a fine tree."

anxiety: 焦慮

閱讀上面的短文，選擇正確答案。

(　　) 1. 　A. worried 　　B.tired 　　C.surprised 　　D.pleased

(　　) 2. 　A. when 　　B.what 　　C.where 　　D.which

(　　) 3. 　A. strangers 　　B.writers 　　C.friends 　　D.fools

(　　) 4. 　A. deep 　　B.easy 　　C.free 　　D.wide

(　　) 5. 　A. everybody 　　B.nobody 　　C.somebody 　　D.none

(　　) 6. 　A. water 　　B.air 　　C.sunlight 　　D.food

(　　) 7. 　A. thought 　　B.talked 　　C.heard 　　D.caught

(　　) 8. 　A. good 　　B.bad 　　C.cheap 　　D.expensive

(　　) 9. 　A. finished 　　B.enjoyed 　　C.wanted 　　D.hated

(　　) 10. 　A. hurt 　　B.changed 　　C.lost 　　D.woke

◀參考譯文▶

　　一個富有的英國農夫有位朋友，這位朋友能培育出非常優良的蘋果樹苗。一天，朋友給了農夫一株好樹苗，讓他帶回家種上。農夫高興地接受了這件禮物，但當他回家後卻不知該往哪裡種。他想：「如果種在路旁，陌生人會偷走蘋果；如果種在田裏，鄰居會在晚上搶走；如果種在房前屋後，自己的孩子會把蘋果摘去。」

　　最後，他把樹苗種在樹林深處、誰也見不到的地方。但沒有陽光，小樹無法生長，所以死掉了。當農夫的朋友聽說這件事後，非常生氣，於是責問農夫為什麼把樹苗種在這樣糟糕的地方。「我能往哪裡種呢？」農夫說，並把自己的擔心告訴朋友。

　　「可那樣總有人能享受到蘋果，」朋友說，「而現在，誰也吃不到蘋果，同時你也失去了一棵優質樹苗。」

---

rob v. 搶劫，盜取：Several people on the train were robbed of their money and jewellery. 列車上有好幾個人被搶去了錢財和首飾。

anxiety n. 擔心，憂慮：There are anxieties over the effects of unemployment. 大家都擔憂失業的後果。

rob v. 搶劫，盜取：Several people on the train were robbed of their money and jewellery. 列車上有好幾個人被搶去了錢財和首飾。

anxiety n. 擔心，憂慮：There are anxieties over the effects of unemployment. 大家都擔憂失業的後果。

◀參考答案▶

1. (D)	2. (C)	3. (A)	4. (A)	5. (B)
6. (C)	7. (C)	8. (B)	9. (B)	10. (C)

Unit 47

| 題材 | 動物世界 | 詞數 | 193 | 建議閱讀時間 | 5 分鐘 |

Animals grow up in different ways. They have lots of lessons to learn.

Some animals are born helpless but their mothers protect them. A newborn kangaroo is the size of a bee. She stays in her mother's safe pouch. She doesn't open her eyes for at least five months. A newborn monkey cannot walk. He is carried by his mother.

Other baby animals can walk soon after they're born. They learn to run with their mothers when danger is near. A baby zebra can run an hour after she is born.

Some baby animals are born in a place that is safe. Other baby animals are born in the open. Baby wolves are born in large holes. A baby elephant is born on open, grassy land. Other elephants make a circle to protect her.

Animals that drink their mothers' milk are called mammals. A mother bear's milk is fatty and rich. Baby bears need lots of fat to keep warm in winter. They have milk for six months. Baby zebras drink milk for six months or more!   As baby animals grow they need solid food. Baby lions eat what their mothers can catch.

kangaroo：袋鼠　pouch：育兒袋　wolves：狼　grassy：多草的　mammals：哺乳動物
fatty：脂肪的　solid：固體的

閱讀上面的短文，選擇正確答案。

(　　) 1.　Which baby animals don't open their eyes for at least five months?
A. Lions.　　　　B. Zebras.　　　　C. Elephants.　　D. Kangaroos.

(　　) 2.　What can't a baby zebra do an hour after she is born?
A. Drink milk.　　　　　　　　B. Run with her mother.
C. Walk by herself.　　　　　　D. Make a circle to protect herself.

(　　) 3.　Which of the following is true according to the passage?
A. Baby wolves are born in the open.
B. Newborn lions only eat solid food.
C. Newborn monkeys can walk but can't jump.
D. Baby bears need lots of fat to keep warm in winter.

【參考譯文】

不同的動物有著不同的成長方式。它們有許多東西要學。

有些動物剛出生時非常無助，但母親可以保護它們。新生的袋鼠只有蜜蜂那麼大，它要待在袋鼠媽媽的育兒袋裏，至少 5 個月才能睜開眼睛。剛出生的猴子不會走路，要由母猴帶著四處活動。

其他動物寶寶剛出生不久就能自己走路。在危險臨近時它們會學著跟媽媽一起奔跑。小斑馬出生一小時後就可以奔跑。

有些動物寶寶出生在安全的地方，有些則出生在野外。狼寶寶出生在寬敞的洞穴中，象寶寶出生在開闊的草原上。象群中的其他成員會圍成一圈保護它。

喝母乳的動物被稱爲哺乳動物。熊媽媽的乳汁富含脂肪，營養豐富。熊寶寶必須儲備充足的脂肪才能在冬季保持溫暖。它們要吃 6 個月的母乳。斑馬寶寶吃母乳的時間爲 6 個月甚至更長！隨著動物寶寶逐漸長大，它們開始需要固體食物了。幼獅可以吃母獅捕食的任何獵物。

【參考答案】

1. (D)　　　2. (D)　　　3. (D)

Unit 48

題材 知識普及　　詞數 181　　建議閱讀時間 4.5 分鐘

People have sailed the world in quite small boats. It is not an easy thing to do. That can be the end of everyone in it. Sometimes the weather gets bad. Accidents can happen easily and quickly.

One family once had an accident. A big fish swam under their boat and bit holes in it. Sea water came in and the boat soon went down. Luckily these people had another small boat—a life-boat, and they all got into the life-boat. They lived and hoped for many days. They ate and slept, and always hoped... At last a ship saved them. How do people live in a very small life-boat for days or weeks even for months? They must be strong in every way. They must have hope, they must want to live.

They cannot drink sea water. Drink a lot of sea water, and you will quickly die. They must catch rain water and drink it. They must also catch fish and birds for food. Life-boats do not often carry a cooker. So people cannot cook their food in the life-boats. Raw fish and bird-meat is not very nice but it is their only food. They must eat raw food, or they will die.

閱讀上面的短文，選擇正確答案。

(　　) 1.　When the boat sank, the life-boat gave the people _____.
　　　　A. food　　　　　B. beds　　　　　C. hope　　　　　D. rain water

(　　) 2.　One family once had an accident at sea, because _____.
　　　　A. their boat met bad weather
　　　　B. a fish bit holes in their boat
　　　　C. the boat hit a big rock and it was broken
　　　　D. none of them knew how to sail the sea

(　　) 3.　People can catch _____ for food and drink at sea in a life-boat.
　　　　A. rain water　　　　　　　　B. fish and birds
　　　　C. both sea water and rain water
　　　　D. both A and B

(　　) 4.　Life-boats do not often carry a cooker, "cooker" here means _____.
　　　　A. something used for cooking　　B. food for cooking
　　　　C. a large box　　　　　　　　　D. a person who cooks food

(　　) 5. Which of the following is NOT true?

A. Sailing around the world in quite small boats is difficult.

B. All the food people have in a life-boat is cooked fish and bird-meat.

C. Anyone who drinks a lot of sea water will die.

D. No one can live for weeks in a life-boat if he is not strong enough.

【參考譯文】

　　有人乘坐小船環遊世界。這可不是一件容易的事。這可能讓參與其中的每個人都送命。有時候，天氣會變糟，事故轉瞬間就會發生。

　　有一家人就曾出過這樣的事故。一條大魚遊到他們的船下，咬了個洞。海水灌了進來，船很快下沉。幸運的是，他們還有另一艘小船——救生艇，他們全都上了救生艇。這麼多天來，他們活了下來，心中祈盼著得救。他們吃了睡，不停地期待著……終於有一艘船救起他們。在很小的救生艇上，人們是怎樣生活幾天、幾周甚至是幾個月的呢？他們必須在各方面都很堅強。他們必須充滿希望。他們必須渴望活著。

　　他們不能喝海水。海水喝多了會很快死去。他們必須接雨水飲用。他們還得捕捉魚、鳥充饑。救生艇上通常沒有爐子。所以人們無法做飯。生魚和鳥肉很不好吃，但他們只有這些。他們必須吃生東西，否則他們會餓死。

---

sail v. 航行，航海：He has sailed the North Sea many times. 他已經幾次橫渡北海。

sink v. （**sank, sunk; sunk, sunken**）（船等）下沉，沉沒：The boat sank to the bottom of the river. 船沉到河底。

life-boat n. 救生艇：The life-boat was called out again during the night. 救生艇夜裏又應召出航。

raw adj. 未煮過的，生的：You can eat carrots cooked or raw. 胡蘿蔔生熟食用皆可。

【參考答案】

1. (C)　　　　2. (B)　　　　3. (D)　　　　4. (A)　　　　5. (B)

Unit 49

題材　人格品質　　詞數　209　　建議閱讀時間　5 分鐘

One day, a boy had a fight with one of his classmates. Then he went to his grandfather and told him his story angrily. "He is really bad," the boy said, "and I __1__ him."

The grandfather said, "__2__ me tell you a story. When I was a boy, I too, sometimes hated others for what they did. But hate will make you feel tired. It doesn't hurt your enemy but only hurt __3__."

As the boy __4__ carefully, the grandfather went on, "There are always two tigers inside my heart. One is good and kind. He gets on well __5__ everything around him. But __6__ is bad and unfriendly. He is full of anger. __7__ the smallest thing will make him angry. He fights with others all the time, and for no __8__. He can't think carefully because he always hates others. It is difficult to live with these two tigers inside my heart. They __9__ try to control me."

The boy looked into his grandfather's eyes and asked, "__10__ tiger always controls you, Grandfather?"

The old man said slowly in a serious voice, "The one that I feed. I always feed the good and kind tiger, so I never hate others and seldom get angry now."

閱讀上面的短文，選擇正確答案。

(　) 1.　A. love　　　　B. hate　　　　C. know　　　　D. enjoy

(　) 2.　A. Make　　　B.Help　　　　C.Let　　　　　D.Ask

(　) 3.　A. myself　　　B.herself　　　C.himself　　　D.yourself

(　) 4.　A. saw　　　　B.felt　　　　　C.talked　　　　D.listened

(　) 5.　A. at　　　　　B.on　　　　　C.with　　　　　D.about

(　) 6.　A. other　　　 B.others　　　C.another　　　D.the other

(　) 7.　A. Even　　　 B.Ever　　　　C.Once　　　　D.Already

(　) 8.　A. time　　　　B.money　　　C.reason　　　 D.place

(　) 9.　A. all　　　　　B. both　　　　C.none　　　　D.neither

(　) 10.　A. Who　　　 B.When　　　 C.Where　　　 D.Which

【參考譯文】

　　一天，一個男孩和同學打了一架。然後他去爺爺那裏，生氣地把這件事告訴他。「他真的很壞，」男孩說，「我恨他。」

　　爺爺說：「我來給你講個故事。小時候，我有時也因為別人的所作所為而恨他們。但恨只會讓你感覺疲憊。恨不會傷害你的敵人，只會傷害自己。」

　　男孩認真聽著，爺爺繼續說道：「我的內心總有兩隻老虎。一只是善良、友好的，它能和周圍的一切融洽相處；但另一只是惡毒、敵意的，它總是充滿怒氣，即使是最小的事情也能讓它生氣。它一直無緣無故地和其他東西爭鬥。它無法仔細思考，因為它總是憎恨其他東西。我心中的這兩隻老虎很難相處，它們都想控制我。」

　　男孩盯著爺爺的眼睛問：「哪只老虎總能控制您呢，爺爺？」

　　老人以嚴肅的口吻緩緩說道：「我餵養的那隻。我總是餵那隻善良、友好的老虎，所以我從不憎恨別人，也很少生氣。」

【參考答案】

1. (B)	2. (C)	3. (D)	4. (D)	5. (C)
6. (D)	7. (A)	8. (C)	9. (B)	10. (D)

Unit 50

題材　知識普及　　　詞數　154　　　建議閱讀時間　4分鐘

Can plants eat people? Probably not, but there are many plants that eat meat. Some of them are big, and they can eat small animals. One famous meat-eating plant is the Venus flytrap.

The Venus flytrap is a very strange plant. It grows in dry parts of the United States. Its leaves are like the pages of a book. They can open and close very quickly. Inside the leaves, there are some small hairs. If a fly touches one of the hairs, the leaf closes quickly. The fly cannot get out. In about half an hour, the leaf presses the fly until it is dead. Then, the plant covers the fly. Slowly, the plant eats the fly.

Why do plants do it? Most plants get what they need from the sun, the air, and the ground. In some places, the ground is very poor. It doesn't have all these important things, especially nitrogen. Animal meat has a lot of nitrogen, so some plants eat meat to get what they need. Let's hope that some of the bigger plants don't get the same idea!

> Venus flytrap：捕蠅草　nitrogen：氮

閱讀上面的短文，選擇正確答案。

(　) 1.　The Venus flytrap is a kind of _____.
A. plant　　　　B. animal　　　　C. meat　　　　D. food

(　) 2.　The Venus flytrap grows in _____.
A. most parts of the world　　B. dry parts of the United States
C. some parts of Africa　　　　D. wet parts of England

(　) 3.　From the passage, we learn that _____.
A. all plants can eat people　　B. all plants can eat animals
C. some plants can eat people　D. some plants can eat animals

(　) 4.　Why do some plants eat animal meat? Because _____.
A. plants are dangerous to animals
B. animals are dangerous to plants
C. plants want to get what they need from animal meat
D. plants want to protect themselves against animals

〔參考譯文〕

　　植物會吃人嗎？很可能不會，但有些植物會吃肉。它們中的某些品種長得很高大，能吃一些小動物。一種著名的食肉植物是捕蠅草。

　　捕蠅草是一種很奇特的植物。它生長在美國的乾旱地區。它的葉子就像書頁。它們可以很快地開合。在葉子裏面有一些小的絨毛。如果蒼蠅碰到了絨毛，葉子就會飛快地合攏。蒼蠅就飛不出去了。大約半小時後，在葉子的擠壓下，蒼蠅死去。然後，葉子把蒼蠅包裹住，並慢慢地把它消化掉。

　　爲什麼植物要這樣做呢？大多數植物都是從太陽、空氣和土壤中獲取自身所需。在某些地方，土地非常貧瘠，土壤中沒有重要的養分，特別是氮。而動物的肉裏含有許多氮，所以有些植物就通過吃肉來獲取所需。但願那些長的高大的植物不要產生同樣的想法吧！

---

trap　n.　陷阱，羅網；圈套：The fox had managed to free itself from the trap. 狐狸設法從陷阱中逃脫了。/The police set a trap for the thief. 警察給小偷設了個圈套。‖ **flytrap** n.　捕蠅草

press　v.　擠，壓，推：Press this button to start the engine.　按這個按鈕發動引擎。/I pressed a coin into the little girl's hanD. 我將一枚硬幣塞進小女孩的手中。

especially　adv.　特別，尤其：He seemed especially tired after school today. 今天放學後，他似乎特別疲憊。

nitrogen　n.　氮：Nitrogen is used in explosives and fertilizers. 氮用於製造炸藥和肥料。

〔參考答案〕

1. (A)　　　　2. (B)　　　　3. (D)　　　　4. (C)

Unit 51

題材　出行方式　　詞數　207　　建議閱讀時間　5分鐘

　　Two years ago, my husband bought me a bicycle. If you live in a town, it is often faster than a car and you don't have to __1__ about parking. You can __2__ it anywhere. As it has a seat at the back and a basket at the front, I can take my small daughter to school, to the library, shopping, __3__ in fact.

　　I use it most in summer when the weather is warm and dry, it can be very unpleasant in winter when it is cold and the rain is __4__ down. It can also be very __5__. You must of course be careful on a bicycle. Accidents are not the only problem though. One day I went shopping and came back to __6__ my front wheel was missing. It was a long __7__ to the bicycle shop! Now I have three strong locks.

　　My husband uses my bicycle sometimes for short journeys. He says it is better than waiting for a bus. He still uses his car for __8__ journeys. But I think that all this __9__ down is making him fat and lazy. On my bicycle I get a lot of __10__ and fresh air, and this makes me feel a lot younger.

unpleasant: 不愉快的

閱讀上面的短文，選擇正確答案。

(　　) 1. 　A. think 　　　　B.talk 　　　　　C.learn 　　　　　D.worry

(　　) 2. 　A. leave 　　　　B.take 　　　　　C.stop 　　　　　D.carry

(　　) 3. 　A. to anywhere 　B.to nowhere 　C.anywhere 　　D.nowhere

(　　) 4. 　A. running 　　　B.dropping 　　C.sinking 　　　D.pouring

(　　) 5. 　A. pleasant 　　　B.dangerous 　　C.unhappy 　　D.interesting

(　　) 6. 　A. tell 　　　　　B.report 　　　　C.telephone 　　D.find

(　　) 7. 　A. road 　　　　B.path 　　　　　C.walk 　　　　D.ride

(　　) 8. 　A. shorter 　　　　　　　　　　 B.more comfortable
　　　　　　 C.longer 　　　　　　　　　　 D.more pleasant

(　　) 9. 　A. sit 　　　　　B.sits 　　　　　C.sat 　　　　　D.sitting

(　　) 10. A. exercise 　　　B.sports 　　　　C.practice 　　D.experience

◖參考譯文◗

　　兩年前，我丈夫給我買了輛自行車。如果你住在小城鎮，自行車通常比汽車快，而且不用擔心停車問題。你可以把它隨便往哪裡一丟。因為這輛車後面有車座，前面有車筐，我能帶著小女兒去上學、去圖書館、購物，實際上哪裡都行。

　　我主要是在夏天天氣溫和乾爽時騎車，而冬天天氣寒冷或大雨傾盆時，騎車就很不舒服了。在這種情況下騎車很危險，當然就得小心謹慎。但事故並不是唯一的問題。有一天我去購物，回來時發現我的前輪不見了。而去自行車商店還有很長的一段路要走！現在，我給自行車上了三把結實的鎖。

　　我丈夫有時也騎我的自行車去附近辦事。他說，這比等公共汽車強。他去較遠的地方時還是開車。但我覺得正是開車時一直坐著把他弄得又胖又懶。通過騎自行車，我得到了許多鍛煉，還能呼吸新鮮空氣，這讓我感覺年輕了許多。

◖參考答案◗

1. (D)	2. (A)	3. (C)	4. (D)	5. (B)
6. (D)	7. (C)	8. (C)	9. (D)	10. (A)

Unit 52

題材　成長故事　　　詞數　259　　　建議閱讀時間　6.5 分鐘

When I was ten, my mother worked all day so I had to take care of my younger brother. At that time my little brother was about four years old and he missed mum all the time.

One day, after I had given him his dinner, he started crying for mum. He was so young and really needed mum. So I dressed him, helped him put on his shoes, carried him on my back and walked out. Soon he fell asleep. About half an hour later, I found that he had lost a shoe while sleeping. I took him off my back and put him down. I knew we needed to find that shoe, for our mother couldn't afford new shoes. We had to go back to find it, so I told my brother to wait right there. A man heard it and stopped me just before I walked off. He asked me, "You are leaving your brother here to find the shoe? What would you do if he is not here when you return?" I did not know how to answer that question. He continued, "<u>It's OK if you can't find the shoe, but it is not OK to lose your brother.</u>" Then he sent us to mum's workplace by taxi.

My whole life I have depended on the kindness of many strangers, I feel <u>regretful</u> that I cannot find them and say thank you. I do not even remember what the man's face looked like, but he taught me a lesson—people are more important than things.

---

mum：媽媽　afford：有能力承擔　workplace：工作地方　kindness：仁慈　regretful：遺憾

閱讀上面的短文，選擇正確答案。

(　　) 1.　Why did the younger brother cry for his mother?
　　　A. Because he was hungry.
　　　B. Because he missed his mother.
　　　C. Because he wanted to play outside.
　　　D. Because he wanted to sleep.

(　　) 2.　What does the underlined word "regretful" in the last paragraph mean?
　　　A. Sorry.　　　B. Excited.　　　C. Happy.　　　D. Angry.

(　　) 3. What did the man mean by saying "It's OK if you can't find the shoe, but it is not OK to lose your brother."?

A. People are more important than things.

B. Things are more important than people.

C. Both the shoe and your brother are important.

D. The shoe is more important than your brother.

(　　) 4. According to the passage, which word can best describe the man?

A. Rude.　　　B. Funny.　C. Silly.　　D. Kind.

【參考譯文】

在我 10 歲時，媽媽整天忙於工作，因此我不得不肩負起照顧弟弟的責任。那時，弟弟大約 4 歲，他一直很想媽媽。

一天，在我安頓他吃過晚飯後，他開始哭著要找媽媽。他那麼小，確實需要媽媽。所以，我給他穿上衣服、鞋子，背著他出門了。很快，他睡著了。大約半小時後，我發現他在睡覺時弄丟了一隻鞋子。我把他從背上放下。我知道我們得找到那只鞋子，因為媽媽買不起新鞋。我們只能回去找鞋子，於是我告訴弟弟在原地等我。一位男士聽到了我的話，在我正要離開時攔住了我。他問我：「你要把弟弟留在這裏，自己去找鞋子嗎？如果你回來時他不在了怎麼辦？」我不知道怎樣回答那個問題。他又說：「如果你沒找到鞋子，那還不要緊，可如果你把弟弟弄丟了，那就不妙了。」然後他用計程車把我們送到了媽媽工作的地方。

我的一生是依靠許多陌生人的好心才走過來的。我因無法找到他們並對他們說聲謝謝而感到遺憾。我甚至不記得那位男士的長相，但他給我上了一課——人比東西更重要。

【參考答案】

1. (B)　　　　2. (A)　　　　3. (A)　　　　4. (D)

Unit 53

題材　名人　　　詞數　164　　　建議閱讀時間　4 分鐘

Florence Nightingale was a famous nurse. She was from a rich family. She took lessons in music and drawing, and read widely. She could speak several foreign languages, and she traveled a lot with her parents. As a child, Florence Nightingale liked visiting sick people and enjoyed helping them. Even when she was traveling in foreign countries, she often visited hospitals. She decided to be a nurse when she grew up.

In 1854, there was a war. During the war, many soldiers were wounded or became ill. The soldiers at the front were in great need of medical care. Florence Nightingale went with thirty-eight nurses to the hospital near the front.

After the war, Florence returned to England. There the Queen congratulated her on her work. But Florence said that her work had just begun. She got people to give money to build the Nightingale Home for Nurses in London, where young girls went to learn nursing.

Florence Nightingale never married. On August 13, 1910, she died quietly in her sleep at the age of ninety. To this day, we still remember her and the wonderful work she did.

---
medical：醫藥的　　congratulated：恭喜

閱讀上面的短文，選擇正確答案。

(　) 1. What was Florence Nightingale?
　　　　A. She was a soldier.　　　　B. She was a nurse.
　　　　C. She was very rich.　　　　D. She was helpful.

(　) 2. Why did Florence Nightingale go to the hospital near the front?
　　　　A. Because the soldiers needed medical care.
　　　　B. Because she wanted to join the army.
　　　　C. Because she wanted to bring the soldiers some food.
　　　　D. Because she wanted to build the Home for Nurses near the front.

(　　) 3.　The Nightingale Home for Nurses in London was to help young girls

　　　　 _____.

　　　　 A. learn nursing　　　　　　B. learn music

　　　　 C. learn drawing　　　　　　D. learn foreign language

(　　) 4.　Can you tell us when Florence Nightingale was born from the passage?

　　　　 A. In 1819.　　　B. In 1910.　　　C. In 1820.　　　D. In 1822.

【參考譯文】

　　弗洛倫斯·南丁格爾是一位著名的護士。她出身于富裕家庭。她學過音樂和繪畫，她的閱讀面也很寬。她能說幾種外語，她和父母去過許多地方。當她還是個孩子的時候，她就喜歡探視病人，還樂於幫助他們。甚至當她在國外旅行時，她也經常去醫院看看。她決心長大後做一名護士。

　　1854 年爆發了一場戰爭。戰爭期間，許多士兵要麼受傷，要麼生病。前線的軍隊急需醫療救助。因此，弗洛倫斯·南丁格爾和 38 名護士奔赴了前線的醫院。

　　戰後，弗洛倫斯返回英國。在那裏，女王表彰了她的工作。但弗洛倫斯說，她的工作才剛剛開始。她勸說人們捐資建設倫敦的南丁格爾護士之家，在那裏，年輕的女孩可以學習護理知識。

　　弗洛倫斯·南丁格爾終生未嫁。1910 年 8 月 13 日，她以 90 歲高齡在睡眠中安靜地死去。直到現在，人們仍在紀念她和她所做出的傑出工作。

---

take　v.　理解，領會；著手學習：take music lessons 上音樂課/take French 學習法語

wound　n.　創傷，傷口　v.　使受傷，傷害‖**wounded**　adj.　受傷的：a wounded soldier 傷兵，傷員 / the wounded （總稱）傷員，受傷者

congratulate　v.　祝賀，向……道喜：I congratulated Sue on passing her driving test. 我祝賀蘇駕駛考試及格。

get　v.　勸說，說服：Get him to see a doctor. 勸他去看醫生。

front　n.　前線：The soldiers retreated from the front. 士兵從前線撤退。

nursing　n.　護理，護理專業：She took up nursing as a career. 她以護理為職業。

【參考答案】

　　1. (B)　　　　　2. (A)　　　　　3. (A)　　　　　4. (C)

Unit 54

| 題材 | 愛心教育 | 詞數 | 175 | 建議閱讀時間 | 4.5 分鐘 |

Marc sat next to me when we were in Hill Junior School. He had a serious __1__ in communicating with people. One always had to guess what he was saying. __2__, most of my classmates did not like to be with him because his hands and shirts were always __3__. I tried to let him know the importance of being clean by __4__ him several times a day to wash his hands. But he just could not understand.

One day, our teacher Miss West walked up to Marc. __5__ saying anything, she took Marc to the washroom. Slowly, Miss West washed his __6__ and told him that he should keep himself clean. She did that every day for one month. __7__, Marc understood.

Miss West's love has given me a good example to __8__ when I am doing my job. I always remember to teach my students by showing them the right __9__ to do things. And most important of all, I always remember to give them more __10__ to learn and to grow up.

---
communicating：溝通　washroom：洗手間

閱讀上面的短文，選擇正確答案。

(　) 1. 　A. question 　　B.problem 　　C.accident 　　D.hobby

(　) 2. 　A. Instead 　　B.However 　　C.Besides 　　D.Except

(　) 3. 　A. dirty 　　B.clean 　　C.new 　　D.old

(　) 4. 　A. talking 　　B.saying 　　C.speaking 　　D.telling

(　) 5. 　A. With 　　B.Without 　　C.After 　　D.Above

(　) 6. 　A. face 　　B.feet 　　C.shirts 　　D.hands

(　) 7. 　A. At last 　　B.At first 　　C.Such as 　　D.So far

(　) 8. 　A. like 　　B.hate 　　C.follow 　　D.think

(　) 9. 　A. ways 　　B.answers 　　C.keys 　　D.food

(　) 10. 　A. money 　　B.work 　　C.fun 　　D.time

【參考譯文】

　　我在希爾初中讀書時，馬克就坐在我旁邊。他在與人溝通方面存在嚴重的問題。別人總得猜測他在說什麼。此外，大多數同學不喜歡和他待在一起，因為他的雙手和襯衫總是很髒。我曾經每天數次提醒他洗手，想使他明白清潔的重要性，但他就是不明白。

　　有一天，我們的老師韋斯特小姐向馬克走去。她什麼也沒說，就把馬克領到洗手間，慢慢地幫他洗手，並告訴他要保持自身清潔。她這樣堅持了一個月，最後，馬克終於明白了。

　　韋斯特小姐的愛給我的工作樹立了學習的榜樣。我一直記得教自己的學生正確的做事方法。最重要的是，我要給他們更多的時間學習和成長。

---

communicate　v. 溝通，聯繫，交往：You don't communicate your ideas clearly in this essay. 你在這篇文章中沒有把觀點表達清楚。

importance　n. 重要（性）：a matter of much importance 相當重要的一件事

【參考答案】

1. (B)	2. (C)	3. (A)	4. (D)	5. (B)
6. (D)	7. (A)	8. (C)	9. (A)	10. (D)

Unit 55

題材　教育　　詞數　170　　建議閱讀時間　4 分鐘

Father came to Jack's bed and sat down beside him. "What kind of day did you have?"

"It was a bad day for me," Jack answered. "I had a fight with Tom. The teacher sent a note home about me. And I talked back to Mother."

"Yes, part of the day was bad," Mr. Brown said. "But tell me about the best thing today."

Jack smiled. "After school I went fishing alone," he said. "I didn't think I would have any pleasure. But I did. I caught a fish!"

"I'm glad you had a good time," Mr. Brown said. "Think about it until you go to sleep. Now I'm going to turn off the light. Happy dreams."

Every night, Jack answers the same question. "What was the best thing that happened to you today?" Every night, Jack thinks about that best thing. Of course he has many happy dreams.

Sometimes he has to think hard to find the best thing. Sometimes it is a very small thing. But he always finds one good thing to think about. This is a good way Jack's father has taught to end his day.

---
talked back：頂嘴

閱讀上面的短文，選擇正確答案。

(　) 1.　The writer mainly wants to tell us _____.
　　　　A. Jack has to think about a question to ask every day
　　　　B. Father's question should be a different one
　　　　C. Father's got a good way to help his son sleep well
　　　　D. Jack doesn't like the question

(　) 2.　Jack thought he had a good time after school that day because _____.
　　　　A. no one went fishing with him
　　　　B. he had a fight with Tom
　　　　C. his teacher didn't come to his home
　　　　D. he caught a fish

（　）3.　From the reading we can know that Jack _____.
　　　A. always has half a bad day and half a good day
　　　B. can always find a good thing to think about
　　　C. often fights with Tom
　　　D. has no bad things to think about every day

（　）4.　Jack's father wants _____ before he goes to sleep every day.
　　　A. him to think about many good things
　　　B. him to remember bad things
　　　C. him to end his day happily
　　　D. to have his son's happy dreams in common

（　）5.　It's clear that to think about a good thing always brings Jack _____.
　　　A. a bad thing　　　　　　　　B. a sleepless night
　　　C. a good tomorrow　　　　　D. a good sleep

【參考譯文】

　　父親走到傑克的床邊挨著他坐下。「今天過得怎麼樣？」

　　「太糟了，」傑克說。「我和湯姆打了一架。老師就寫便條告我的狀，為此我還和媽媽頂嘴。」

　　「這只能說明一天中的部分時間過得很糟，」布朗先生說。「說說今天最開心的事。」

　　傑克笑了。「放學後，我一個人去釣魚，」他說。「我原以為不會有什麼收穫。但不是這樣，我釣到了一條魚！」

　　「我很高興你過得愉快，」布朗先生說。「睡覺前你就想這件事。現在我要關燈了。做個好夢。」

　　每天晚上，傑克都要回答同樣的問題。「今天發生在你身上最高興的事是什麼？」每天晚上他都要想著最高興的事入睡。當然，他做了許多美夢。

　　有時候，他要很費一番腦筋才能找到最開心的事。有時候，是一件很小的事。但他總能找到值得回味的事情。這就是傑克的父親教給他的結束一天的好辦法。

note　n.　短箋，便條：leave a note to tell sB. to do sth. 留條子告訴某人做某事

talk back　頂嘴，反駁：Don't talk back to your grandmother when she is giving you advice, you should be polite to your elders. 奶奶規勸你時不要對她頂嘴，對長輩要有禮貌。

sleepless　adj.　不眠的，失眠的，醒著的：Late in the night, sleepless and troubled, he got up and went for a walk. 深夜，他憂心忡忡，難以成寐，索性起床散步。

common　adj.　共有的，共同的 ‖ **in common** 共用，共享：Real friends should have everything in common. 真正的好朋友什麼東西都應該共享。

【參考答案】

1. (C)　　　　2. (D)　　　　3. (B)　　　　4. (C)　　　　5. (D)

Unit 56

| 題材 | 網絡禮儀 | 詞數 | 124 | 建議閱讀時間 | 3 分鐘 |

Imagine you receive an e-mail that looks something like this: ARE YOU GOING TO CLASS TODAY? How does __1__ this message make you feel? Why did the sender use __2__ capital letters? Was he or she angry, __3__ did that person just __4__ to turn off the "Caps Lock" on the computer? This e-mail "sounds" like the __5__ is shouting because using all capital letters in an e-mail is __6__ the way that people shout online.

Knowing when and when not to __7__ capital letters is just one __8__ of online etiquette.

Don't do anything online that you wouldn't do in __9__ life. Don't use information that someone else has written, and __10__ it's yours. Do share your knowledge of the Internet with others.

---
sender：發信者　capital letters：大寫字母　Caps Lock：大寫鎖定　etiquette：禮儀

閱讀上面的短文，選擇正確答案。

(　) 1.　A. reading 　　B. typing 　　C. watching 　　D. leaving

(　) 2.　A. some 　　B. all 　　C. any 　　D. none

(　) 3.　A. but 　　B. or 　　C. and 　　D. so

(　) 4.　A. start 　　B. begin 　　C. forget 　　D. remember

(　) 5.　A. writer 　　B. worker 　　C. nurse 　　D. student

(　) 6.　A. hardly 　　B. carefully 　　C. silently 　　D. usually

(　) 7.　A. copy 　　B. believe 　　C. double 　　D. use

(　) 8.　A. mistake 　　B. advice 　　C. example 　　D. game

(　) 9.　A. digital 　　B. real 　　C. quiet 　　D. healthy

(　) 10.　A. speak 　　B. tell 　　C. talk 　　D. say

【參考譯文】

　　假如你收到一封電子郵件，裏面的內容類似於下面這句話：你-今-天-去-上-學-嗎？讀了這封郵件會讓你產生怎樣的感覺？爲什麼發件人所有的字母都用了大寫？他或她生氣了嗎？還是那個人只是忘了關閉鍵盤上的「大寫鎖定」？這封電子郵件看起來就像是寫信人正在大喊大叫，因爲在電子郵件中，所有的字母都大寫通常是表示那個人在網上大喊。

知道什麼時候應該、什麼時候不應該使用大寫字母只是網絡禮儀的一個例子。

不要做任何現實生活中你不會去做的事。不要使用別人寫下的東西，並謊稱是自己的。把你的網絡知識和他人分享。

---

capital　n. 大寫字母：He wrote the title in capitals. 他用大寫字母寫下題目。

caps　n.〔縮寫〕（=capital letters）大寫字母：Caps Lock 大寫鎖定

etiquette　n. 禮儀：Etiquette requires a man to rise when a woman enters the room. 按禮節，女士進入室內時男士應起立。

【參考答案】

1. (A)	2. (B)	3. (B)	4. (C)	5. (A)
6. (D)	7. (D)	8. (C)	9. (B)	10. (D)

Unit 57

題材 熱點話題　　**詞數** 221　　**建議閱讀時間** 5.5 分鐘

To understand why the Earth is warming up, first of all, we need to understand why <u>it</u> is warm. Our planet is covered with atmosphere. Sunlight passes through the atmosphere and reaches the Earth. The Sun heats up the Earth's surface. When the heat rises into the air, it is stopped by some special gases in the atmosphere like CO2, the heat returns to the Earth and keeps it warm.

Power stations and cars release so many greenhouse gases every day. So we can help stop global warming by using less electric things such as turning off lights when we leave a room, asking our parents to turn down the heating in our house to save energy. We can also stop global warming by finding other ways of transportation. For example, ride a bicycle or walk instead of going by car. Another way to help stop global warming is to plant and care for trees. Because trees take in CO2, they are our best friends when fighting against global warming.

The problem of global warming cannot be solved in a day. It may take a long time to find clean energy, such as wind energy. It may take a long time to plant the trees again we are cutting down. But every little thing each person can do to save energy and our forests will help. Think about our planet. Think about ways we can help make the Earth a safe and comfortable place for the future.

---
atmosphere：大氣　surface：表面　release：釋放　greenhouse：溫室
transportation：交通

閱讀上面的短文，選擇正確答案。

(　　) 1.　The underlined word "it" means _____ in the first paragraph.
　　　　A. the heat　　　　　　　　B. the Earth
　　　　C. the atmosphere　　　　　D. the sunlight

(　　) 2.　_____ ways are mentioned to stop global warming according to the second paragraph.
　　　　A. Two　　　　B. Four　　　　C. Three　　　　D. Five

(　　) 3. Which of the following is NOT true?

A. Everybody can help save energy and our forests.

B. The problem of global warming can not be solved.

C. To find clean energy will help solve the problem of global warming.

D. The writer wants us to pay attention to the problem of global warming.

(　　) 4. Which is the best title of this passage?

A. Why is the Earth warming up

B. When can we stop the Earth from warming up

C. How can we stop the Earth getting warmer

D. How long will it take to stop the Earth getting warmer

【參考譯文】

　　想要搞清楚爲什麼地球溫度會逐漸升高，首先要瞭解地球溫暖的原因。我們的星球被大氣層覆蓋著。陽光穿過大氣層直射到地球，從而使地球表面溫度上升。當熱量上升、進入大氣的時候，又被大氣層中諸如 CO_2 之類的特殊氣體所阻礙，於是熱量又返回地球，從而使地球保持溫暖。

　　每天，發電廠和汽車都釋放出很多溫室氣體。所以，如果我們少用電器，就可以爲防止地球變暖出一份力，比如在離開房間時隨手關燈，讓父母調低家中的暖氣設備以節約能源。我們還可以尋找其他出行方式，比如騎自行車或步行出門而不是乘車。還有一個辦法是植樹、護樹，因爲樹木能夠吸收 CO_2，在防止地球變暖的戰鬥中，它們是我們最得力的戰友。

　　解決全球變暖的問題不可能一蹴而就。我們需要花很長時間去尋找諸如風能之類的清潔能源，我們需要花很長時間將砍倒的樹木重新栽上。但如果每個人都在節約能源、保護森林方面做一點努力，就會對地球有所幫助。凡事多想想這個星球，多想想辦法，給我們的地球母親營造一個安全而舒適的未來。

---

release v. 釋放：Oxygen from the water is released into the atmosphere. 水中的氧氣被釋放到大氣中。

global adj. 全球的：global changes in climate 全球氣候變化

transportation n. 交通：The price includes hotels and transportation. 該價格包括住宿和交通費用。

【參考答案】

1. (B)　　　　2. (C)　　　　3. (B)　　　　4. (C)

Unit 58

題材 獲取知識	詞數 145	建議閱讀時間 3.5 分鐘

Food is very important. Everyone needs to __1__ well if he or she wants to have a strong body. Our minds also need a kind of food. This kind of food is __2__. We begin to get knowledge even when we are very young. Small children are __3__ in everything around them. They learn __4__ while they are watching and listening. When they are getting older, they begin to __5__ story books, science books... anything they like. When they find something new, they love to ask questions and __6__ to find out the answer.

What is the best __7__ to get knowledge? If we learn __8__ ourselves, we will get the most knowledge. If we are __9__ getting answers from others and do not ask why, we will never learn well. When we study in the right way, we will learn more and understand __10__.

閱讀上面的短文，選擇正確答案。

(　) 1. 　A. sleep 　　　B.read 　　　C.drink 　　　D.eat

(　) 2. 　A. sport 　　　B.exercise 　　C.knowledge 　D.meat

(　) 3. 　A. interested 　B.interesting 　C.weak 　　　D.better

(　) 4. 　A. everything 　B.something 　　C.nothing 　　D.anything

(　) 5. 　A. lend 　　　B.read 　　　　C.learn 　　　D.write

(　) 6. 　A. try 　　　　B.have 　　　　C.think 　　　D.wait

(　) 7. 　A. place 　　　B.school 　　　C.way 　　　　D.road

(　) 8. 　A. on 　　　　B.with 　　　　C.to 　　　　D.by

(　) 9. 　A. often 　　　B.always 　　　C.usually 　　D.sometimes

(　) 10. A. harder 　　B.much 　　　　C.better 　　　D.well

【參考譯文】

　　食物非常重要。如果一個人想擁有健壯的身體就必須吃好。我們的頭腦也需要一種食物。這種食物就是知識。我們很小的時候就開始接受知識。小孩子對身邊的每件事都感興趣。他們在觀察和傾聽的時候就已經學到了東西。隨著年齡的增長，他們開始閱讀故事書、科學書等，總之是他們喜歡的一切。當他們發現了新奇的東西，他們喜歡問問題並努力尋找答案。

　　獲取知識的最好方法是什麼？如果我們獨立自主地學，我們就會得到最多的知識。

如果我們總是從他人那裏尋找答案，而不去問爲什麼，我們就永遠也學不好。當我們用正確的方法學習時，我們將學到更多，理解得更好。

---

by oneself 獨立地；全靠自己地：Baby walked by himself this morning — all the way from that mat to the table. 寶寶今天早晨自己走起路來——他從蹭鞋墊那邊一直走到餐桌旁。

【參考答案】

1. (D)	2. (C)	3. (A)	4. (B)	5. (B)
6. (A)	7. (C)	8. (D)	9. (B)	10. (C)

Unit 59

題材　健康　　　詞數　155　　　建議閱讀時間　4分鐘

Do you feel a little sleepy after lunch? Well, that's normal. Your body naturally slows down then. What should you do about it? Don't reach for a coffee! Instead, take a nap.

It's good to have a daily nap. First of all, you are more efficient after napping. You can remember things better and make fewer mistakes. Also, you can learn things more easily after taking a nap. A nap may increase your self-confidence and make you more active. It may even cheer you up.

Here are some suggestions you can follow about taking a nap. First, take a nap in the middle of day, about eight hours after you wake up. Next, a 20-minute nap is the best. If you sleep too long, you may fall into a deep sleep. After waking from a deep sleep, you will feel worse. Also, you should set an alarm clock. That way, you needn't worry about you will oversleep, and you can fully relax during your nap.

Now, the next time you feel sleepy after lunch, don't get stressed. Put your head down, close your eyes, and take a nap.

normal：正常的　nap：小睡　efficient：有效率的　self-confidence：自信
suggestion：建議

閱讀上面的短文，選擇正確答案。

(　　) 1.　After napping, you will _____.
　　　A. make more mistakes　　　B. be less self-confident
　　　C. get stressed out　　　D. learn things more easily

(　　) 2.　If you _____, you will fully relax yourself.
　　　A. take a nap as long as you can
　　　B. take a nap at about five o'clock in the afternoon
　　　C. fall into a deep sleep
　　　D. set an alarm clock to make sure you won't oversleep

(　　) 3.　The passage mainly tells us _____.

A. it's good to drink some coffee

B. how to increase our self-confidence

C. the importance of taking a nap

D. to set an alarm clock before napping

(　　) 4.　The passage is about _____.

A. sports　　　　B. health　　　　C. music　　　　D. shopping

【參考譯文】

　　午餐後你是不是感覺有點困乏？是的，這很正常。按照規律，那時的身體需要放鬆。對此，你應該做些什麼呢？不要伸手拿咖啡！相反，你需要小憩一下。

　　每天打一會盹是很有益處的。首先，小睡後你會變得效率更高。你能夠更有效地記住事情，同時少犯錯誤。當然，小睡也能讓你學習起來更輕鬆。它能提高你的自信，讓你變得更活躍，甚至讓你的精神振奮起來。

　　關於小睡，這裏有一些可供參照的建議。首先，小睡應該安排在一天的中間時段，也就是起床後 8 小時左右。其次，時間最好 20 分鐘。如果睡的時間太長，就會進入深度睡眠。從深度睡眠中醒來，你會覺得更疲憊。還有，最好設定一下鬧鐘。那樣的話，你就不必擔心睡過頭，而且可以充分放鬆。

　　好了，下一次如果午餐後覺得昏昏欲睡，不用那麼緊張。低下頭、合上眼，小憩一下吧。

---

nap　n.　小睡，打盹：take an afternoon nap 午後小睡一下

efficient　adj.　高效的：The city's transport system is one of the most efficient in Europe. 這個城市的交通系統是歐洲最高效的系統之一。

self-confidence　n.　自信：He can only develop self-confidence if he is told he is good and clever. 只有當人們誇他乖巧、聰明時，他才會產生自信心。

【參考答案】

1. (D)　　　2. (D)　　　3. (C)　　　4. (B)

Unit 60

題材　知識普及　　　詞數　164　　　建議閱讀時間　4 分鐘

November 9 is a time for us to learn a lot more about fire. This is what to do in a fire:

1. Shout out. Shout as loudly as you can, because people may be asleep.

2. Call 119. Never try to put out a fire yourself. Tell 119 where you are and what is on fire.

3. Keep down close to the floor. There is less smoke down there, so it's easier to breathe and see where you are going.

4. Test the door. If the door is cool, open it carefully. If the door is hot, do not open it! Try to find a different way out.

5. Get out. Do not stop to pick up anything. A fire can become very big in a few seconds!

6. Don't use the lift. Always use the stairs. The lift may go wrong and keep you inside.

7. Don't go back. Even if you have left your pet or favorite toy inside, do not go back for it. Animals have a very good sense of smell. They often get out of buildings before people.

閱讀上面的短文，選擇正確答案。

(　　) 1.　According to the passage, when something is on fire, you must _____ at once.
　　　　A. look for your pet　　　　　　B. telephone 119
　　　　C. put out the fire yourself　　　D. call 120

(　　) 2.　The passage tells us that we can _____ in a fire.
　　　　A. use the lift
　　　　B. open the hot door and go out
　　　　C. try to put out a fire ourselves
　　　　D. shout as loudly as possible

(　　) 3.　You should keep down close to the floor because _____.
　　　　A. people may be asleep
　　　　B. the firemen can find you easily
　　　　C. there is less smoke down there
　　　　D. you should look after your things carefully

(　　) 4.　If the door is hot, we should _____.
　　　　A. open it and get out　　　　B. find another way out
　　　　C. stop to pick up something　D. go back for something

(　　) 5.　The lift is dangerous in a fire because _____.
　　　　A. it is too small　　　　　B. it may go wrong
　　　　C. it may keep you inside　　D. both B and C

◖參考譯文◗

11 月 9 日讓我們對火有了更多的瞭解。下面就説説碰到火災怎麼辦：

1. 大聲呼救。盡可能大聲地呼救，因爲人們可能還在睡覺。

2. 撥打 119。不要想著自己滅火。告訴 119 你的位置以及什麼東西著火了。

3. 儘量伏在地板上，那裏的煙較少，你比較容易呼吸，也能看清逃生的方向。

4. 推門試試。如果門不燙，小心翼翼地打開它。如果門很燙，不要開門！儘量尋找別的出口。

5. 離開著火點。不要停下來拿東西。小火也可能在幾秒鐘後變成大火。

6. 不要使用電梯。儘量走樓梯。電梯可能出故障，把你困在裏面。

7. 不要返回。即使你的寵物或最喜愛的玩具還在裏面，也不要回去找。動物對煙很敏感。它們常常趕在人的前面離開建築物。

---

go wrong　（機器等）發生故障，出毛病：The machine has gone wrong—I can't get it to stop!
　　這機器出了故障——我無法讓它停下來！

sense　n.　感官，官能：We have five senses. They are our senses of sight, smell, hearing, touch and taste. 我們有五種官能，它們是視覺、嗅覺、聽覺、觸覺和味覺。

◖參考答案◗

1. (B)　　　　2. (D)　　　　3. (C)　　　　4. (B)　　　　5. (D)

Unit 61

題材　工作　　　　　詞數　168　　　　建議閱讀時間　3 分鐘

Sarah left school at eighteen, went to college and then worked at a computer company. Four years later, she got a new job as a manager in British Airways. This is what she told us about her job:

"My office is at Heathrow Airport, but I spend 60% of my time in the air. I teach air-hostesses and help them with any problem. I also go to lots of meetings."

"My hours are usually from 8 a.m. to 4 p.m., but sometimes I work from 1 p.m. to 9 p.m. At work, the first thing I do is to check plane times on my computer and then I speak with some of the air-hostesses."

"Sometimes I go on long flights to check how the air-hostesses are doing. That's my favorite part of the job, but I like office work, too. Travelling can be hard work. When I get back from a long trip, all I can do is to eat something and then go to bed! I don't make much money, but I'm happy with British Airways and want to stay there and continue to travel."

air-hostess：空中小姐

閱讀上面的短文，選擇正確答案。

(　　) 1.　Sarah's first job was _____.
　　　　A. at a college　　　　　　B. at a computer company
　　　　C. in British Airways　　　D. at Heathrow Airport

(　　) 2.　Sarah does most of her work _____.
　　　　A. in meetings　　　　　　B. in the computer room
　　　　C. in the office　　　　　　D. in airplanes

(　　) 3.　Most days, Sarah starts work at _____.
　　　　A. 8 a.m.　　　B. 1 p.m.　　　C. 4 p.m.　　　D. 9 p.m.

(　　) 4.　The first thing Sarah does after a long trip is to _____.
　　　　A. go to bed　　　　　　　B. have a meal
　　　　C. go to a meeting　　　　　D. go to the office

(　　) 5. Sarah would like to ＿＿＿＿.
      A. make more money　　　　B. stop travelling
      C. go to college again　　　　D. stay in the same job

【參考譯文】

　　莎拉 18 歲時離開中學上大學，後來到了一家電腦公司工作。4 年後，她在英國航空公司謀得一份經理的新工作。下面就是她給我們講述的工作情況：

　　「我的辦公室在希斯羅機場，但我 60% 的工作時間都在飛機上。我給空姐們上課，並幫她們解決各種問題。我還要參加許多會議。」

　　「我的工作時間通常是從上午 8 點到下午 4 點，但有時候是從下午 1 點到晚上 9 點。上班的時候，我做的第一件事就是在電腦上核對航班時間，然後和一些空姐談話。」

　　「有時候我也飛長線，為的是檢查空姐們的工作情況。這是我最喜歡的工作內容之一，但我也喜歡辦公室的工作。旅行非常辛苦。當我結束長途旅行後，我能做的就是吃東西，然後上床睡覺！雖然我賺錢不多，但我很喜歡英國航空公司，並且想待在這兒繼續旅行。」

---

airway　n.　航空公司：British Airways 英國航空公司

flight　n.　飛行：Too much money has been spent on flight. 在坐飛機旅行上花的錢太多了。

check　v.　檢查，核對：She checked her work every time before handing it in. 她每次交作業之前先檢查一遍。

make money 賺錢：They made a lot of money last year. 去年他們賺了很多錢。

【參考答案】

   1. B　　　　　2. D　　　　　3. A　　　　　4. B　　　　　5. D

Unit 62

題材　犯罪　　　詞數　186　　　建議閱讀時間　4 分鐘

Your honor!

Let me say a few words for myself. What they have told you is not true. I was not trying to kill anyone, and it was hardly possible to try to kill three strong young men at the same time. I didn't have anything to kill people that night and was quite alone. I didn't know them and needn't hate them.

I was attacked by them, and I knocked one of them down, it's true, but I was made to do it, or I might be killed by them. I did this not because I hated the white men as they said. I just had to do so. While I was beaten in the dark street by the three men, a policeman came, caught me and then took me here.

I know why I was beaten. I have just moved into a house next to these white men. I have felt that I am not welcome and I have tried to be quiet. I think, as an American, I have the right to choose where to live. If I'm guilty, what makes me guilty is my color opposite to theirs and I can't enjoy justice. Yet, I'm not guilty. This is all I want to say. Thank you, your honor.

guilty：有罪的　　opposite：相反的　　justice：公平、正義

閱讀上面的短文，選擇正確答案。

(　) 1. What color was the speaker?
　　　　A. Black.　　　　B. White.　　　　C. Brown.　　　　D. Yellow.

(　) 2. Why did he speak for himself?
　　　　A. He wanted to live in the house next to the whites.
　　　　B. He was not trying to kill anyone.
　　　　C. He wanted to show he was not guilty.
　　　　D. He wanted to show he didn't hate the whites.

(　) 3. The speaker was caught because _____.
　　　　A. the policeman wanted to save him
　　　　B. he was a black and was fighting with the whites
　　　　C. he killed the three men in a dark street
　　　　D. one of the whites was knocked down by the speaker

(　　) 4.　What's the right order of the story?

　　　　a. The speaker said something for himself.

　　　　b. The three men said something.

　　　　c. The speaker knocked down one of the three men.

　　　　d. The speaker was beaten by the three men.

　　　　e. He was caught by the policeman.

　　　　f. The speaker moved into a house near the whites.

　　　　A. a b f d c e　　B. b a f c d e　　C. f d c e b a　　D. f c d e a b

【參考譯文】

法官大人！

　　讓我為自己辯解幾句。他們告知於您的並非事實。我不想殺任何人，而且要想同時殺死三個壯漢幾乎是不可能的。那天晚上，我沒有攜帶任何殺人工具，而且我是孤身一人。我不認識他們，對他們也沒有仇恨。

　　我受到了他們的攻擊，於是我撞倒了其中的一人，這是事實，但我是被迫的，否則，我就有可能被他們殺掉。我這樣做，並非像他們所說的那樣，是因為我憎恨白人。我只是被迫如此。當我在黑暗的街道中被三個人暴打時，一位警察過來抓住了我，並把我帶到了這裏。

　　我知道自己為什麼挨打。因為我剛剛搬進緊鄰這三個白人的房子裏。我已經感到自己不受歡迎，並且已經努力保持安靜。作為一名美國人，我認為自己有選擇居住地的權利。如果我有罪，那麼成立我罪名的原因是因我和他們相反的膚色，而且我享受不到公正的待遇。然而，我沒有罪。我想說的就是這些。謝謝您，法官大人。

Your honor　（對法官或某些高級官員的尊稱）閣下，先生

attack　v.　襲擊，攻擊：The disease attacked her suddenly. 疾病突然向她襲來。

guilty　adj.　有罪的，犯罪的：The jury found him guilty of murder. 陪審團認為他犯謀殺罪。

justice　n.　正義，公正，公平：All men should be treated with justice. 人人都應受到公正的待遇。

opposite　adj. 相反的，對立的：She hurried away in the opposite direction. 她匆忙地朝相反方向跑去。/His political position is opposite to ours. 他的政治立場與我們的對立。

【參考答案】

　　1. A　　　　2. C　　　　3. C　　　　4. C

Unit 63

題材 動物　　詞數 169　　建議閱讀時間 3分鐘

The flying fox is not a fox at all. It is an extra large bat that has got a fox's head, and that feeds on fruit instead of insects. Like all bats, flying foxes hang themselves by their toes when at rest, and travel in great crowds when out flying. A group will live in one spot for years. Sometimes several hundreds of them occupy a single tree. As they return to the tree toward sunrise, they quarrel among themselves and fight for the best places until long after daylight.

Flying foxes have babies once a year, giving birth to only one at a time. At first the mother has to carry the baby on her breast wherever she goes. Later she leaves it hanging up, and brings back food for it to eat. Sometimes a baby bat falls down to the ground and squeaks for help. Then the older ones swoop down and try to pick it up. If they fail to do so, it will die. Often hundreds of dead baby bats can be found lying on the ground at the foot of a tree.

quarrel：吵架　breast：胸部　squeak：尖叫　swoop：飛撲

閱讀上面的短文，選擇正確答案。

(　　) 1. The passage tells us that there is no difference between the flying fox and the ordinary bat in _____.
A. their size
B. their appearance
C. the kind of food they eat
D. the way they rest

(　　) 2. Flying foxes tend to _____.
A. double their number every year
B. fight and kill a lot of themselves
C. move from place to place constantly
D. lose a lot of their young

(　　) 3. At daybreak every day flying foxes begin to _____.
A. fly out toward the sun
B. look for a new resting place
C. come back to their home
D. go out and look for food

(　　) 4. Flying foxes have fights _____.

    A. to occupy the best resting places

    B. only when it is dark

    C. to protect their homes from outsiders

    D. when there is not enough food

(　　) 5. How do flying foxes care for their young?

    A. They only care for their own babies.

    B. They share the feeding of their young.

    C. They help when a baby bat is in danger.

    D. They often leave home and forget their young.

【參考譯文】

飛狐根本不是狐狸。它是一種頭部類似狐狸的特大號蝙蝠，以水果而不是昆蟲為生。和所有的蝙蝠一樣，飛狐休息時用腳趾倒掛住身體，外出時成群結隊。一群飛狐會在一個地方生活多年。有時幾百隻飛狐會同時佔據一棵樹。當飛狐在天亮前返回這棵樹時，它們之間開始發生爭吵，為佔領最好的位置打鬥到天亮。

飛狐一年一胎，一胎一子。起初，飛狐媽媽無論去哪裡，都會將小飛狐掛在自己胸前。後來飛狐媽媽會讓小飛狐自己倒吊著，然後取食回來喂它。有時小飛狐會掉在地面上，並發出吱吱的求救聲。這時，年長的飛狐會俯衝而下，盡力將它們救起。如果救助不成功，小飛狐就會死掉。人們經常可以發現，樹底下躺著數以百計死掉的小飛狐。

---

squeak v. 發出短而尖的聲音：The mouse squeaked in the corner. 老鼠在角落裏吱吱地叫著。

swoop v. 飛撲；俯衝：The hawk swooped down and seized the rabbit. 那只鷹從空中飛撲而下抓起了兔子。

【參考答案】

    1. D   2. D   3. C   4. A   5. C

Unit 64

題材 實驗　　　詞數 176　　　建議閱讀時間 4分鐘

Put an ice cube from your fridge into a glass of water. You have a piece of string 10 centimeters long. The problem is to take out that piece of ice with the help of the string. But you must not touch the ice with your fingers.

You may ask your friends to try to do that when you are having dinner together. There is a saltcellar on the table. You must use salt when you carry out this experiment.

First you put the string across the piece of ice. Then put some salt on the ice. Salt makes ice melt. The ice round the string will begin to melt. But when it melts, it will lose heat. The cold ice cube will make the salt water freeze again.

After a minute or two you may raise the piece of string and with it you will raise your piece of ice!

This experiment can be very useful to you. If, for example, there is ice near the door of your house, you must use very much salt to melt all the ice. If you don't put enough salt, the water will freeze again.

---

ice cube：冰塊　fridge：冰箱　string：繩子　saltcellar：鹽瓶　melt：融化

閱讀上面的短文，選擇正確答案。

(　) 1. We must use _____ when we carry out this experiment.
A. a fridge　　B. some food　　C. a table　　D. some salt

(　) 2. How long will it take to carry out this experiment?
A. More than three minutes.　　B. Five minutes or so.
C. Only one minute or two.　　D. About ten minutes.

(　) 3. What is the task of this experiment?
A. Put the ice cube into the glass of water with the help of the string.

B. Take out the ice cube in the glass of water with the help of the string.

C. Take out the ice cube in the glass of water with your fingers.

D. Put some salt on the ice cube and then put the string across it.

(　　) 4.　How many things at least are used in this experiment?
　　　　A. Three.　　　　B. Four.　　　　C. Six.　　　　D. Seven.

(　　) 5.　We can learn something about _____ from the passage.
　　　　A. physics　　　B. biology　　　C. chemistry　　　D. maths

【參考譯文】

　　從冰箱裏拿出一塊冰塊，放進裝有水的杯子裏。找一根 10 公分長的細繩。問題是：用這根繩子把冰塊取出來。但不能用手碰那塊冰塊。

　　如果你正和朋友一起吃晚飯，你可以請他也試著做做。桌子上有一隻鹽碟。當你做這個實驗時，肯定會用到鹽。

　　首先，你把繩子橫放在冰塊上。然後在冰塊上撒一些鹽。鹽使冰融化。繩子周圍的冰也開始融化。冰融化時，熱量降低，較冷的冰塊會使鹽水再次凍結。

　　一兩分鐘後，你拿起繩子，同時也就拿起了吊著的冰塊！

　　這個試驗對你非常有用。比如，如果你家門前有冰，你必須灑很多鹽把冰化掉。如果放的鹽不夠，水會再次結冰。

---

cube　n.　立方體，立方體物：cube sugar 方糖/ice cubes 冰塊

string　n.　線，繩：a （piece of）　string 一根繩子/a ball of string 一團線

saltcellar　n.　（餐桌上的）鹽碟，鹽瓶

melt　v.　融化，熔化：When we got up in the morning, the snow had melted. 我們早上起床時，雪已融化。

freeze　v.　結冰，凝固：Leave the heating on when you're away or the pipes will freeze. 不在家時也得開著暖氣，要不然水管要凍住了。

【參考答案】

1. D　　　　2. C　　　　3. B　　　　4. B　　　　5. C

Unit 65

題材 家庭教育　　詞數 227　　建議閱讀時間 5分鐘

Dear Ellen,

I have never written a letter to a newspaper before. I have just never felt the need to do such a thing. I have always felt I was quite able to do everything by myself. But now I have to say I was wrong. Sometimes you really need help in life, I guess. And that's why I'm writing this letter to you.

I have a happy family. I love my children and they love me. I'm the mother of three children. I know well how to bring up children, and two of them are already over twenty, so it is nothing new for me. But now I have a serious problem: the telephone problem. My little son's just seventeen, and I feel he should do lots of homework right now, but he doesn't seem to be interested in it. He can happily spend three or four hours at a time on the phone every day, and say nothing important. And <u>he sees red</u> if you ask him to put down the phone. But Ellen, my husband is a doctor and his patients can't call him. My eldest son works for a newspaper. He needs to use the telephone, too. And as you know, we just can't pay for it.

What can I do? And don't tell me to talk to him. We've tried that and it doesn't work. But this is really a big problem in our life. I have tried everything I can think of. You're my last hope. Please tell me what I can do!

Yours

Ann Green

閱讀上面的短文，選擇正確答案。

(　　) 1.　Mrs. Green wrote to Ellen because _____.
　　　A. she often asked others for help
　　　B. she thought she was a great mother
　　　C. she thought only Ellen could help her
　　　D. she could not get on well with her son

(　　) 2.　_____ made the telephone problem.
　　　A. Her first child　　　　B. Her second child
　　　C. Her third child　　　　D. All her children

(　　) 3. What might Mrs. Green's son say on the phone?
A. Something about his lessons.　B. Something he was interested in.
C. Something important.　D. Nothing important.

(　　) 4. What does the underlined sentence "he sees red" mean in this passage?
A. He feels sorry.　B. He feels happy.
C. He becomes sad.　D. He becomes angry.

◖參考譯文◗

親愛的埃倫：

　　我以前從未給報社寫過信，我覺得沒有必要這樣做。我一直以為自己完全能夠獨立處理每件事。但現在我得說，我錯了。我想，有時候，人在生活中確實是需要幫助的。這就是我寫信給你的原因。

　　我有一個幸福的家庭。我愛孩子們，他們也愛我。我是三個孩子的母親。我很明白怎樣撫養孩子。其中兩個孩子已經20多歲了，他們沒有什麼新問題讓我操心。但現在，我有一個嚴重的問題，它是關於電話的。我的小兒子剛剛17歲，我覺得他現在應該做許多家庭作業，但他對此似乎不感興趣。他能興致勃勃地每天連續三四個小時打電話，說些雞毛蒜皮的事。如果你要求他放下電話，他還會跟你發脾氣。埃倫，我丈夫是一名醫生，在這種情況下，他的病人就無法跟他通話了。我的大兒子在報社工作，他也需要使用電話。而且你知道的，太多的電話費我們承受不起。

　　我該怎麼辦呢？不要告訴我跟他談談。我們已經試過了，沒有用的。但這確實是我們生活中的一個大問題。我已經嘗試了我能想到的所有方法。你是我最後的希望。請告訴我該怎麼做。

安·格林敬上

guess v. 猜想，判斷：Without a clock he could only guess what time it was. 沒有鐘，他只好猜是什麼時間。

serious adj. 嚴肅的，令人擔憂的：You look very serious: is anything the matter?你看上去很嚴肅，發生什麼事了？

see red 發怒：When he spoke in that way, I saw red and struck him. 當他那樣說話時，我就氣得火冒三丈，動手打了他。

◖參考答案◗

1. C　　　2. C　　　3. B　　　4. D

Unit 66

題材 建議　　　**詞數** 228　　　**建議閱讀時間** 4 分鐘

You can always find the advice column in the school newspaper. No one knows who writes it. The students think their teacher does, but it might be a student using a false name. The students enjoy thinking up problems for the advice column. Here are some of them and their answers.

Tommy: I'm always late for school. I try not to be, but I can't. Please advise me what to do.

Clever Monkey: You are late for school probably because you go to bed too late. My advice to you is to go to bed earlier, buy a clock to wake you up on time.

Sara: I was brought up by my grandparents and began to live with my parents three years ago for a better study environment. They love me; I can see this in their eyes. But I don't know how to show my love for them. What can I do to let them know I love them back?

Clever Monkey: If you feel the need to show your love for your parents, that's great. Make sure you remember their birthdays and buy them cards and presents. Try to spend time with your parents. Tell them how you feel. Try to enjoy your life. Your parents want you to be happy—if you are happy, they will be happy, too.

Molly: I'm one of the best students in my class. But I always make some mistakes which I should not make. And now, I'm afraid to see my teachers. I just don't know how to face them. Can you tell me how I can solve this problem?

Clever Monkey: The first thing you need to do is to relax. Worrying about your studies is not going to help. If you have any difficulty, tell your teachers. No teacher is going to get angry with a student who wants to improve himself.

---

advice column：建議欄　relax：休閒、放鬆

閱讀上面的短文，選擇正確答案。

(　) 1.　The Clever monkey thinks that Tommy is always late for school because he _____.

    A. dislikes his school　　　　　　B. goes to bed late

    C. watches TV too much　　　　　D. wants to stay at home all day

(　) 2.　What's Sara's problem?

    A. She can't fall asleep at night.

    B. She always makes mistakes in exams.

    C. She doesn't know how to face her teachers.

    D. She doesn't know how to show her love back to her parents.

(　) 3.　What doesn't the Clever Monkey want Sara to do?

    A. To remember her parents' birthdays.

    B. To spend time with her parents.

    C. To make money for her family.

    D. To tell her parents how she feels.

(　) 4.　We can know from the passage that Molly _____.

    A. is often late for school

    B. does well in her studies

    C. is very weak in all her lessons

    D. is very happy

(　) 5.　What's the main idea of this passage?

    A. The students use false names in the school.

    B. The students don't like the advice column.

    C. The clever monkey in the advice column.

    D. The advice column in the school newspaper.

【參考譯文】

　　你總是能在校報上發現建議欄。沒人知道是誰寫的。學生們認為是他們的老師寫的，但也有可能是某個學生用假名所寫。學生們喜歡針對建議欄設想問題。以下是一些學生的提問及得到的回答。

　　湯米：我老是遲到。我不想這樣，但又做不到。請告訴我該怎麼辦。

　　聰明猴：你遲到很可能是因為睡覺太晚。我對你的建議是：早點睡覺，再買一只能準時叫醒你的鐘。

　　莎拉：我是爺爺奶奶帶大的，三年前，為了讓我有一個更好的學習環境，我開始和父母一起生活。他們愛我，從他們的眼神中我能看到這一點。但我不知道怎樣向他們表示我的愛。我怎樣做才能讓他們明白我也愛他們呢？

　　聰明猴：如果你意識到需要向父母表達愛，那很棒。你一定要記住他們的生日，並給他們買賀卡和禮物。儘量花時間和他們待在一起。告訴他們你的感受。享受你們在一起的時光。你的父母想讓你幸福——你幸福他們就幸福。

　　莫莉：我是班裏成績最好的學生之一，但我總犯一些不該犯的錯誤。現在，我害怕見老師。我只是不知道怎樣面對他們。你能告訴我如何解決這個問題嗎？

　　聰明猴：你要做的第一件事是放鬆。擔心學業沒什麼幫助。如果你有困難，告訴你的老師。沒有一個老師會對想進步的學生生氣。

solve	v.	解決：We have solved the math problem. 我們已解答出了這個數學題。
relax	v.	放鬆，使鬆弛：The music will help to relax you. 這音樂將有助於使你放鬆。
		/Let's stop working and relax for an hour. 咱們停止工作休息一小時吧。
dislike	v.	不喜歡，討厭：I really dislike flying. 我真的不喜歡坐飛機。

【參考答案】

1. B　　　　2. D　　　　3. D　　　　4. B　　　　5. D

Unit 67

題材　熱點新聞　　　詞數　168　　　建議閱讀時間　3 分鐘

Two months after beginning the new work hours, good results have been reported in Kyoto. Now work starts at 9 in the morning, an hour later than before. But people still go back home at 6 in the afternoon.

"With one more hour's sleep every day, I feel much better," said a worker there.

Now people still work as long as before, but not from 8:00 to 6:00. They go to work an hour later, but have a shorter lunch break. In the past they had two hours for lunch, but now they have only one hour. Many people welcome the new work hours. "Why do we have to waste a lot of time in the middle of the day and rush in the early morning?"

Two months ago, many people got up at 6:30 a.m. every workday and left home at 7:00 a.m. It usually took them about an hour to get to the office from home. Morning time was always like a battle.

The use of the new work hours is just beginning. It is important to follow the office hours in the world. Most foreign countries have "nine-to-five" work hours. If we don't change, there will be problems. When Japanese start working at 8 a.m., foreigners haven't begun business yet. But when they are busy working at noon, Japanese are still on break. So some people think that it is the right time to change.

---

battle：戰鬥

閱讀上面的短文，選擇正確答案。

(　　) 1.　What are the new work hours in Kyoto?
　　　　A. 9 a.m. to 5 p.m.　　　　　B. 8 a.m. to 5 p.m.
　　　　C. 9 a.m. to 6 p.m.　　　　　D. 9 a.m. to 7 p.m.

(　　) 2.　How long do people in Kyoto work every workday now?
　　　　A. Eight hours.　B. Seven hours.　C. Nine hours.　　D. Six hours.

(　　) 3.　How is people's life different now?
　　　　A. They have less time to sleep.
　　　　B. The work hours are shorter.

C. They have less time for lunch.

D. They waste a lot of time in the middle of the day.

(　　) 4.　How long have people used the new work hours?

A. For two months.　　　　　B. For a week.

C. For two weeks.　　　　　D. For a month.

(　　) 5.　Why do people use the new work hours?

A. Because they like to work long hours.

B. Because the old work time is not good enough.

C. Because they want to change the work hours in other countries.

D. Because traffic was too busy in the early morning.

【參考譯文】

在京都，新的工作時間啟用兩個月後，良好的效果已經顯現。現在的工作時間是從上午9點開始，比以前推後了一個小時。但人們還是在下午6點回家。

「每天多一個小時的睡眠時間，我感覺好多了，」那裏的一位工人說。

現在，人們的工作時間還和以前一樣長，但不是從早上8點到下午6點了。他們的上班時間晚了一個小時，但中午休息時間變短了。過去，他們有兩個小時的午餐時間，但現在只有一個小時。許多人歡迎這種新的工作時間。「為什麼我們一定要浪費大量的時間在中午上，而弄得早上匆匆忙忙呢？」

兩個月前，每逢工作日，許多人早上6點半起床，7點鐘離家。他們從家趕到單位通常要用一個小時。早上的時間就像是一場戰鬥。

新工作時間的啟用只是一個開始。效仿國際工作時間是很重要的。大多數國家都使用「朝九晚五」的工作時間。如果我們不作改變，就會產生問題。當日本人在早上8點開始工作時，外國人還沒有上班。但當他們在中午忙碌時，日本人卻在休息。因此，有些人認為，改變適逢其時。

result n. 結果，成效：We worked all day, but without any result. 我們工作了一整天，但沒什麼成效。

break n. 短暫休息，休假：The coach told us to take a break for five minutes. 教練叫我們休息五分鐘。

rush v. 匆匆趕往，倉促行事：They rushed up the stairs. 他們沖上樓梯。

battle n. 戰鬥，戰役：They won the first battle but still they lost the war. 他們第一仗打贏了，但還是輸了整場戰爭。

【參考答案】

1. C　　　　2. A　　　　3. C　　　　4. A　　　　5. B

Unit 68

題材　招聘　　詞數　193　　建議閱讀時間　4 分鐘

A famous foreign company in Taiwan wanted a clerk for its public relation department.

A beautiful girl with a master's degree went through a lot of challenges and her name was on the list. In the final stage she faced an interview together with another girl. Both of them were outstanding, not only in looks but also in education.

The girl was successful in the interview. It seemed that she would get the chance. At last the examiner asked her, "Can you come to the office next Monday?" Shocked by the unexpected question, the beautiful girl couldn't make a decision at the moment, so she said, "I have to talk with my parents before I give an answer." The examiner felt surprised but said calmly, "If so, let's wait till you are ready."

The next day, the girl came to tell the examiner that her parents had agreed to let her begin work next Monday. But the examiner said regretfully, "Sorry, another suitable candidate has got the job. You had better try another place." The beautiful girl was surprised. She asked for an explanation and was told, "What is needed here is a person who knows her own mind."

That was how a good opportunity right under the nose of a beautiful girl ran away.

---

relation：關係　challenge：挑戰　shock：震驚　unexpected：意外的
suitable：適合的　candidate:候選人　explanation：解釋　opportunity:機會

閱讀上面的短文，選擇正確答案。

(　　) 1.　The beautiful girl wanted to ask her parents for advice because _____.
　　　A. she didn't like the job
　　　B. she didn't expect the examiner would ask such a question
　　　C. she didn't want to answer the question
　　　D. her parents would be angry if she didn't ask them

(　　) 2. We can learn from the passage that _____.

A. the company lost its best clerk

B. no girl got the job

C. the other girl who failed at the last interview might get the job

D. the examiner was very pleased with the girl

(　　) 3. The examiner regarded _____ as the most important.

A. a person's confidence

B. a person's knowledge

C. a person's age

D. a person's beautiful looks

(　　) 4. The underlined phrase **"*right under the nose of*"** probably means _____.

A. 就在鼻子下　　　　　　　B. 想要得到的

C. 沒有把握的　　　　　　　D. 就在眼前的

(　　) 5. The best title for the passage above might be _____.

A. Make Decisions with Your Parents

B. A Successful Interview

C. Use Your Own Mind

D. Answer the Examiner's Question Quickly

【參考譯文】

一家知名在台外資公司要為其公關部招聘一名職員。

一位擁有碩士學位的漂亮女孩通過層層考驗，最終進入備選人員名單。在最後階段，她和另外一個女孩共同接受面試。她們兩人都很優秀，不僅是外表，也包括學歷。

這個女孩在面試時表現出色，似乎即將贏得工作機會。最後，面試官問她：「下週一你能來上班嗎？」這個出人意料的問題讓女孩措手不及，她沒有立刻作出決定，而是說：「在給出答復前，我得先和父母商量一下。」面試官感到很驚訝，但他平靜地說：「如果是這樣，那就等你準備好了再說吧。」

第二天，女孩過來告訴面試官，她的父母已經同意她下週一上班。但面試官遺憾地說：「抱歉，另一位合適的候選人已經獲得了這份工作，你最好到別處試試吧。」女孩很驚訝，她要求給出解釋，結果被告知：「我們這裏需要的是有獨立思考能力的人。」

這個故事講的是：漂亮女孩眼皮底下的好機會是怎樣溜走的。

public relation　n.　公共關係：Giving money to local charities is good for public relations. 捐款給本地慈善機構有助於促進公共關係。

master's degree　n.　碩士學位

candidate　n.　選手，候選人：We have some very good candidates for the post. 這個職位的申請人當中有幾個挺不錯的人選。

【參考答案】

1. B　　　　　2. C　　　　　3. A　　　　　4. D　　　　　5. C

Unit 69

題材　朋友　　詞數　160　　建議閱讀時間　3 分鐘

Many teenagers feel that the most important people in their lives are their friends. They believe that their family members don't know them as well as their friends do. In large families, it is quite often for brothers and sisters to fight with each other and then they can only go to their friends for some ideas.

It is very important for teenagers to have one good friend or a group of friends. Even when they are not with their friends, they usually spend a lot of time talking among themselves on the phone. This communication is very important in children's growing up, because friends can discuss something. These things are difficult to say to their family members.

However, parents often try to choose their children's friends for them. Some parents may even stop their children from meeting their good friends. Have you ever thought of the following questions?

Who chooses your friends? Do you choose your friends or your friends choose you? Have you got a good friend your parents don't like?

Your answers are welcome.

---
communication：溝通；通訊　attitude：態度

閱讀上面的短文，選擇正確答案。

(　　) 1.　Many teenagers think that _____ can understand them better.
　　　A. friends　　　B. brothers　　　C. sisters　　　D. parents

(　　) 2.　_____ is very important to teenagers.
　　　A. To make friends　　　B. Communication
　　　C. To stop meeting friends　　　D. Both A and B

(　　) 3.　When teenagers have something difficult to say to their parents, they usually _____.
　　　A. stay alone at home
　　　B. fight with their parents
　　　C. discuss it with their friends
　　　D. go to their brothers and sisters for help

（　　）4.　The sentence "***Your answers are welcome***" means "_____".

A. You are welcome to discuss the questions with us

B. We've got no idea, so your answers are welcome

C. Your answers are always right

D. You can give us all the right answers

（　　）5.　Which of the following is the writer's attitude?

A. Parents should choose friends for their children.

B. Children should choose everything they like.

C. Parents should understand their children better.

D. Teenagers should only go to their friends for help.

【參考譯文】

　　許多青少年覺得，在他們的生命中，最重要的人是朋友。他們認為，家人並不像朋友那樣瞭解他們。在大家庭中，兄弟姐妹打架是常有的事，事後他們只能找朋友出主意。

　　對青少年來說，有一個或是一批好朋友是很重要的。即使他們不和朋友在一起，他們也會花很多時間通過電話和他們交談。溝通對兒童的成長非常重要，因為有了事情可以和朋友一起討論。這些事情很難對家人說出口。

　　然而，父母常常想替孩子們選擇朋友。有些父母甚至會阻撓他們的孩子見自己的好朋友。你想到過下面這些問題嗎？

　　是誰選擇你的朋友？是你選擇朋友，還是朋友選擇你？你有父母不喜歡的好朋友嗎？

　　歡迎給出你的答案。

---

teenager　n.　青少年：a young teenager of fourteen　14 歲的少年

fight　n.　打架，搏鬥；爭吵：Don't get into a fight at school, will you? 不要在學校打架，好嗎？

communication　n.　交際，溝通：Good communication is important for business. 良好的溝通對做生意來說很重要。

discuss　v.　討論，商量：I've something of great importance to discuss with you. 我有些非常重要的事同你商量。

attitude　n.　態度：She shows a very positive attitude to her work. 她的工作態度很積極。

【參考答案】

　　1. A　　　　2. D　　　　3. C　　　　4. A　　　　5. C

Unit 70

| 題材 | 自然 | 詞數 | 190 | 建議閱讀時間 | 4分鐘 |

If we find a bird nest, we will have a good place of observing and knowing about birds.

Birds sit on eggs and take care of their baby birds from April to June. Because the baby birds are too young to leave the nest, mothers often leave and come back to the nest during the time to look for food. So it is good to observe birds. When we observe birds, we'd better hide ourselves in a close place to the nest, and it's better to use binoculars.

But how to make a bird nest? It's very easy. If you want to make one, please follow these:

Making a nest: A good nest must be very fine, strong, thick and easy.

a) Each nest must have six boards. Don't make the boards too slippery.

b) Dig a small hole in the front of the nest as a door. The "door" is from 3cm to 5cm. So the bird can fly in or out easily.

c) Make sure the rainwater doesn't go into the nest.

d) One piece of the boards should be easy to open.

e) Please don't forget to color the nest.

---

observe：觀察　binoculars：望遠鏡　slippery：滑溜

閱讀上面的短文，選擇正確答案。

(　　) 1. The most important thing in observing birds is to _____.
　　　　A. look for a place near the nest　B. climb trees
　　　　C. write down notes every day　　D. make a bird nest

(　　) 2. When we're observing birds, we have to hide ourselves to _____.
　　　　A. look after them
　　　　B. use the binoculars
　　　　C. make them do everything as usual
　　　　D. catch the birds at last

（　）3.　If we make the nest too slippery, _____.
　　A. it's not strong
　　B. it's not easy to make
　　C. it's not very beautiful
　　D. it's very difficult for birds to hold or stand on

（　）4.　We should leave a hole in the front of the nest so that _____.
　　A. we can clean the nest　　B. the birds can fly in or out
　　C. we can hang it easily　　D. it's easy to make

【參考譯文】

如果我們發現一個鳥巢，我們就有了觀察和瞭解鳥類的絕佳地點。

4 月到 6 月是鳥類孵化並照顧雛鳥的時候。因爲雛鳥太小，不能離巢，所以這段時間母鳥就得經常離巢尋找食物，然後再返回。所以這時候很適合觀察鳥類。當我們觀察鳥類時，最好把自己隱藏在靠近鳥巢的地方，並儘量使用雙筒望遠鏡。

但怎樣製作鳥巢呢？很簡單。如果你想做一個，按下面的步驟做就行了：

製作鳥巢：好的鳥巢必須很精緻、結實、厚實、方便。

a）每個鳥巢必須有 6 塊木板。木板的表面不能太光滑。

b）在巢的正面挖一個小洞作門。「門」的大小爲 3 到 5 公分。這樣，鳥就能方便地飛進飛出。

c）確保雨水不會灌進鳥巢。

d）有一塊木板應容易打開。

e）不要忘了給鳥巢塗上顏色。

nest n.　（鳥）巢；窩；穴：A rat took the egg while the mother bird was away from the nest. 趁雌鳥不在巢裏，一隻老鼠把蛋偷走了。

observe v.　看到，注意到；觀察，觀測：We observed that it had turned cloudy. 我們注意到天轉陰了。

binoculars n.　雙筒望遠鏡：He focused his binoculars on the building in the distance. 他把雙筒望遠鏡對準遠處那座建築物。

slippery adj.　滑的，使人滑跤的：The soap was smooth and slippery. 這肥皂很滑溜。

board n.　木板，紙板：The old house needed new floor boards. 這座舊房子要換上新地板。

【參考答案】

1. A　　　　2. C　　　　3. D　　　　4. B

Unit 71

題材 哲理故事　　**詞數** 173　　**建議閱讀時間** 3.5 分鐘

　　A group of frogs were traveling through the forests, but unluckily two of them fell into a hole. The other frogs tried to help them. When they saw how __1__ the hole was, they cried to the two frogs that they could not be saved. The two frogs didn't __2__ and tried their best to jump up out of the hole. The other frogs __3__ saying that they were sure to die. __4__, one of the two frogs, who heard what the other frogs were saying, __5__. Then he fell down and died.

　　The other frog, however, __6__ to jump as hard as he could, and at last made it. When he __7__, the other frogs asked, "Didn't you hear us?" The frog, who had a poor __8__, explained, "I thought you were encouraging me all the time."

　　The story teaches us a __9__: There is power of life and death in the tongue. An __10__ word to those who are down can help them out while a discouraging word can kill them.

unluckily：不幸地　encouraging：鼓勵的

閱讀上面的短文，選擇正確答案。

(　) 1. 　A. small 　　　B. deep 　　　C. big 　　　　D. wide
(　) 2. 　A. care 　　　B. refuse 　　　C. insist 　　　D. think
(　) 3. 　A. kept 　　　B. finished 　　C. practiced 　　D. stopped
(　) 4. 　A. Luckily 　　B. Finally 　　C. Suddenly 　　D. Happily
(　) 5. 　A. went on 　　B. ran away 　　C. jumped out 　D. gave up
(　) 6. 　A. happened 　B. continued 　C. planned 　　D. wanted
(　) 7. 　A. got out 　　B. ran away 　　C. got off 　　　D. woke up
(　) 8. 　A. smelling 　　B. eyesight 　　C. hearing 　　D. looking
(　) 9. 　A. way 　　　B. skill 　　　　C. sentence 　　D. lesson
(　) 10. A. interesting 　B. exciting 　　C. excellent 　　D. encouraging

【參考譯文】

　　一群青蛙正結隊穿過森林，不幸的是，其中兩隻掉進了洞裏。其他青蛙想幫助它們，可當它們看到洞很深時，就對那兩隻青蛙喊道，它們沒法救它倆。那兩隻青蛙沒有理會，竭盡全力想跳出洞來。其他青蛙不停地說它們必死無疑。最終，一隻青蛙聽到這樣的說法後放棄了，它跌入洞底摔死了。

　　然而，另一隻青蛙卻不停地竭盡全力向上跳，最後它居然成功了。當它出來後，其他青蛙問道：「難道你沒有聽見我們的喊話？」這隻聽力不好的青蛙解釋說：「我以爲你們一直在鼓勵我呢。」

　　這個故事告訴我們一個道理：語言有一種決定生死的力量。對於那些身處困境的人，一句鼓勵的話就能幫助他們振作起來，而一句洩氣的話則能置其於死地。

make it 成功做到（某事）：I was thirty-even and I wanted to make it as a writer. 我那時 37 歲，我想成為一位成功的作家。

tongue n. 語言：The stranger spoke in a foreign tongue. 那個陌生人講外語。

【參考答案】

1. B	2. A	3. A	4. B	5. D
6. B	7. A	8. C	9. D	10. D

Unit 72

| 題材 | 故事 | 詞數 | 250 | 建議閱讀時間 | 5分鐘 |

A man was selling medicines at a fair. At first he sold bottles of a cure for colds for just a dollar a bottle.

Many people wanted to buy it and the man's young assistant moved quickly through the crowd collecting money and handing out bottles of the cold cure.

Then, when he had a big crowd, the man held up a very small bottle.

"And now, ladies and gentlemen," he shouted, "here is the medicine you have been waiting for. The cure for old age. Drink just one bottle of this and you will live forever."

"And, ladies and gentlemen," the man continued, "I'm not going to charge you a hundred dollars a bottle for this wonderful medicine. I'm not going to charge you fifty dollars a bottle. I'm not going to charge you twenty-five dollars a bottle. No, ladies and gentlemen, I'm going to charge you just ten dollars a bottle. Think, my friends, for ten dollars you can live forever."

Most of the people in the crowd did not believe this.

One person shouted, "if it will make you live forever, why don't you drink it?"

Then another person cried, "Yes, you look as if you're at least sixty years old."

"Thank you, sir, thank you," the man replied, "I'm so glad you said that. My real age is three hundred and twenty-nine."

The crowd laughed at this but there were still a few people who wanted to believe the man. One of them spoke to the man's assistant as she passed by. "Is that true," he asked, "that he's three hundred and twenty-nine?"

"Don't ask me," the assistant said, "I've only worked for him for a hundred and fifty years."

---

forever：永遠

閱讀上面的短文，選擇正確答案。

(　　) 1.　What did the man sell at first?

A. A cure for colds.

B. Empty bottles.

C. A cure for old age.

D. A medicine that made people live forever.

(　　) 2.　Why didn't the people believe the man was selling medicine that could cure old age?

A. The medicine was too cheap.

B. The medicine was too expensive.

C. He looked quite old himself.

D. He didn't look honest.

(　　) 3.　How old did the man selling medicine say he was?

A. At least sixty.

B. Over three hundred.

C. A hundred and fifty.

D. He didn't say.

(　　) 4.　How much did the man charge for the cure for old age?

A. One dollar a bottle.

B. Twenty-five dollars a bottle.

C. Ten dollars a bottle.

D. Fifty dollars a bottle.

(　　) 5.　We can know from the passage that _____.

A. the man was very honest

B. the assistant was also very honest

C. the man was very stupid

D. neither the man nor the assistant was honest, for they were cheating people

【參考譯文】

一個人在市集上賣藥。開始時，他賣的是一美元一瓶的感冒藥。

許多人想買，賣藥人的年輕助手飛快地在人群中穿梭，把錢收進來，把藥遞過去。

後來，賣藥人身邊聚了一大群人，這時，他拿出一個小瓶子。

「聽著，女士們，先生們，」他喊道，「這裏有一種你們期待已久的藥──消除衰老的藥，只要喝上一瓶，你們就能永生。」

　　「女士們，先生們，」他繼續說，「這種神奇的藥，我不打算賣 100 美元一瓶，我也不打算賣 50 美元一瓶，我還不打算賣 25 美元一瓶。不，女士們，先生們，我只打算賣 10 美元一瓶。朋友們，想想吧，只要 10 美元，你們就能永生了。」

　　人群中的大多數不相信他的話。

　　有一個人喊道：「如果這種藥能讓人長生不老，為什麼你不來一瓶？」

　　接著另一個人喊道：「就是，你看上去至少六十歲了呢。」

　　「謝謝你，先生，謝謝，」賣藥人答道，「我很高興你這麼說。我的真實年齡是 329 歲。」

　　聽到這裏，人群中發出哄笑，但還是有幾個人願意相信他說的話。其中有一個人趁著賣藥人的助手從身旁經過時，問她道：「他活了 329 歲，這是真的嗎？」

　　「別問我，」助手說，「我在他這裏只工作了 150 年。」

---

fair　n.　集市；展銷會：The village has a fair once a month. 那個村莊每月有一次集市。

charge　v.　收費：He was charged heavily for it. 他為它支付了一大筆錢。

【參考答案】

　1. A　　　　　2. C　　　　　3. B　　　　　4. C　　　　　5. D

Unit 73

題材　成長故事　　　詞數　247　　　建議閱讀時間　5分鐘

I think I've always been interested in food. My grandparents lived on a farm in Lincolnshire and had a good __1__. She made fantastic English food; her roast beef was out of this world. I used to love going down to the __2__ and watching her work, and I learned a lot from her. I realized that I wanted to be a cook when I was about 12. When other boys __3__ to do sports after school, I helped with cooking at home.

By the time I was 15, I had __4__ to be a cook. However, I knew my parents wouldn't allow me to be a cook. I had to tell them about it __5__. I told them that I wanted to do a cookery course for fun, and I stayed for a month in a hotel in Torquay. I enjoyed it so much that I couldn't put off telling my parents any longer, __6__ I brought the subject up one night over dinner. __7__ there was silence, and then my father asked me why. I explained that cooking was __8__ painting a picture or writing a book. Every meal was a work of creation. I could see that my father disagreed, but he was not __9__. He just looked at me and smiled. My mother kissed me.

And now I have my own restaurant, and it goes well. I can see they are __10__ me. However, my grandfather thinks I'm mad to give up farming.

---
roast：燒烤　cookery：烹飪的　creation：創造

閱讀上面的短文，選擇正確答案。

(　) 1.　A. farmer　　　B. painter　　　C. cook　　　D. nurse

(　) 2.　A. restaurant　B. hotel　　　　C. farm　　　D. kitchen

(　) 3.　A. chose　　　B. refused　　　C. hated　　　D. failed

(　) 4.　A. decided　　B. agreed　　　C. managed　　D. turned

(　) 5.　A. easily　　　B. softly　　　C. slowly　　　D. quietly

(　) 6.　A. but　　　　B. so　　　　　C. or　　　　　D. for

(　) 7.　A. At first　　B. At last　　　C. At least　　D. At times

(　) 8.　A. with　　　　B. like　　　　C. about　　　D. above

(　) 9.　A. patient　　B. satisfied　　C. quiet　　　D. angry

(　) 10.　A. proud of　B. sorry for　　C. friendly to　D. strict with

【參考譯文】

　　我覺得我總是對食物感興趣。我的祖父母住在林肯郡的一個農場裏，他們有個好廚子。她給我們做美味的英式食物。她做的烤牛肉簡直不像人間應有的東西。我過去很喜歡去廚房看她做飯，我還從她那兒學到很多東西。大約 12 歲時，我意識到我想成為一名廚師。每當其他男孩放學後選擇做各種運動時，我則在家幫忙做飯。

　　15 歲時，我下定決心要成為廚師。然而，我知道父母是不會允許我做廚師的。我得慢慢跟他們解釋。我告訴他們我想學一門烹飪課程，只是為了消遣，於是我在托基的一家旅館待了一個月。我非常喜歡這門課程，迫不及待地想告訴父母我的想法。於是，一天晚上，我在飯桌上把這個想法提了出來。開始是一陣沉默，接著父親問我原因。我解釋說烹飪就像繪畫或寫書一樣。每道菜都是創作的成果。我能看出父親不同意，但他沒有生氣。他只是看著我笑了笑。母親親吻了我。

　　現在，我有了自己的餐廳，而且營運良好。我能看出他們為我而驕傲。然而，祖父卻認為我放棄農場的工作是瘋了。

---

fantastic　adj. 極出色的，了不起的：a fantastic meal 一場盛宴

put off 推遲，拖延：She put the trip off until next week.她把旅行延遲到下周。

subject　n. 話題：He was clearly embarrassed to talk about his private life, and tries to change the subject.他顯然不好意思談論自己的私生活，所以儘量轉移話題。

【參考答案】

1. C	2. D	3. A	4. A	5. C
6. B	7. A	8. B	9. D	10. A

Unit 74

題材　旅遊景點　　　詞數　186　　　建議閱讀時間　4分鐘

Few people would be foolish enough to walk among lions and other wild animals. Today you can drive safely through wild animal country, if you keep your car windows closed. There are a number of such open-space zoos in the United States. The first was opened in 1967 in Florida. It is called Lion Country Safari.

Lion Country Safari has 650 acres full of wild African animals. There are many lions and about 350 other animals, such as elephants, giraffes, zebras, rhinos, ostriches, and chimps. To keep visitors safe, there are a few rules—no cloth-top convertibles, all windows closed, and no getting out of cars.

For those who like to get closer to the animals, there is a petting section where there are baby animals only. It's safer in that way.

cloth-top convertibles：布頂敞篷車　petting section：愛撫區

閱讀上面的短文，選擇正確答案。

(　　) 1. The best title is _____.
A. Walking with Wild Animals　　B. Elephants and Lions
C. Follow the Rules　　　　　　　D. A Drive-in Zoo

(　　) 2. One thing NOT allowed in Lion Country Safari is _____.
A. hard-top cars B. closed windows
C. cloth-top convertibles　　　　D. wild animals

(　　) 3. In Lion Country Safari there are _____.
A. 640 elephants　　　　　　　　B. 35 animals
C. 1967 giraffes　　　　　　　　D. many lions

(　　) 4. Leaving car windows open in the Lion Country Safari would be _____.
A. fun　　　　　　　　　　　　　B. safe
C. dangerous　　　　　　　　　　D. wise

【參考譯文】

　　幾乎沒有人會傻到要和獅子或其他種類的野獸同行。但是現在，如果將車窗關牢，你就可以安全地在野生動物王國駕車穿行。在美國，有很多這樣的開放式動物園。第一個這樣的動物園於 1967 年在佛羅裏達州開張，它被稱作獅子王國。

　　獅子王國占地 650 英畝，放養了很多來自於非洲的野生動物，其中包括大量獅子和大約 350 種其他動物，比如大象、長頸鹿、斑馬、犀牛、鴕鳥和黑猩猩等。爲了保證遊客的安全，動物園有一些規定——不能乘坐布頂的敞篷車，必須關閉所有車窗，不能走出車外等。

　　對於那些想近距離接觸這些動物的遊客，園區專門設立了愛撫區。那裏只有幼小的動物，這樣就安全多了。

safari　n.　（可駕車四處遊覽的）野生動物園

acre　n.　英畝（=4 047 平方米）：The building stands in nine acres of ground. 這幢建築占地 9 英畝。

convertible　n.　（篷子可折疊的）敞篷汽車

pet　v.　愛撫：The cat purred when she was petted. 受到愛撫時，那只貓發出嗚嗚的叫聲。

【參考答案】

　　1. D　　　　　2. C　　　　　3. D　　　　　4. C

Unit 75

題材 業餘愛好　　　　**詞數** 202　　　　**建議閱讀時間** 4 分鐘

My hobby is playing chess—one of the greatest games in the world. My mum taught me __1__ to play when I was seven years old. She __2__ me every time for the first year. But then, on my eighth birthday, I won for the first time. Now I am always the __3__ between us.

It takes about a day to learn the rules. __4__ if you want to be good, you have to practice for years. You don't need much to play chess — just a chess set and someone to play with. Chess sets __5__ be very cheap, or quite expensive. Some people collect chess sets as a hobby, but I __6__ to play.

There is a chess club in our school. We meet every week to play each other. I am the best __7__ in the club, and the captain of the school chess team. This year we __8__ the All England Schools' Championship. I had to go up on stage in front of the whole school to collect the prize.

I'm saving up my money to buy a chess __9__. It's very good for practice. In that way I'll __10__ have someone to play with, and I'm sure I'll make more progress.

閱讀上面的短文，選擇正確答案。

(　) 1.　A. what　　　　B. why　　　　C. how　　　　D. where
(　) 2.　A. hit　　　　　B. lost　　　　C. beat　　　　D. fought
(　) 3.　A. loser　　　　B. winner　　　C. sender　　　D. ruler
(　) 4.　A. And　　　　B. So　　　　　C. Yet　　　　D. But
(　) 5.　A. can　　　　　B. must　　　　C. should　　　D. will
(　) 6.　A. want　　　　B. wish　　　　C. prefer　　　D. choose
(　) 7.　A. player　　　　B. fan　　　　C. leader　　　D. learner
(　) 8.　A. received　　　B. won　　　　C. lost　　　　D. owned
(　) 9.　A. computer　　B. book　　　　C. dictionary　D. game
(　) 10.　A. sometimes　B. sometime　　C. always　　　D. seldom

【參考譯文】

我的業餘愛好是下西洋棋——這是世界上最偉大的運動之一。在我七歲時，媽媽教會了我怎樣玩。頭一年，她每次都贏我。但後來，在我八歲生日時，我第一次贏了。現在，我們倆下棋總是我贏。

學習規則要花一天的時間。但如果想下好，就得練習多年。下西洋棋所需不多——一副棋和一個對手足矣。一副西洋棋的價錢可以很便宜，也可以很貴。有些人還有收集西洋棋的愛好，但我更喜歡下棋。

我們學校有一個西洋棋俱樂部。我們每週都聚會一次切磋棋藝。我是俱樂部裏最好的選手，還是校棋隊的隊長。今年，我們獲得了全英校際聯賽的冠軍。我必須站在領獎臺上面對全校師生領獎。

我正在攢錢買一台西洋棋電腦，這對練習很有好處。那樣的話，我就不用總是找人對弈了，而且我堅信自己會取得更大的進步。

---

set n. (一)套，(一)副：a chess set 一副西洋棋

championship n. 冠軍地位：Two more points and the championship will be his! 再得兩分，冠軍就是他的了！

stage n. 舞臺：Some children are dancing on the stage. 一些孩子正在舞臺上跳舞。

【參考答案】

1. C	2. C	3. B	4. D	5. A
6. C	7. A	8. B	9. A	10. C

Unit 76

題材　周圍的人　　詞數　186　　建議閱讀時間　4分鐘

I always thought that a man who was wise and good would become rich, but this year I have learned that this is not always true.

I learned this from my teacher. He is both wise and good, but is not rich at all, for being a teacher, he doesn't have a good income. He may be able to get more money if he gives up teaching for business. But he is so proud of being a teacher that he takes pleasure in helping young people.

He stays at school from morning till late afternoon and works very hard. He always smiles at us when we go to ask him for help. <u>He is kinder to us than anyone whom I've ever known</u>. I think it must be easier to learn history or maths than to learn how to become such a man. He scolds us when we do something wrong, but it teaches us to try to do better.

We all wish to study with him as long as possible, but that may be impossible. Some of us may become doctors, some become businessmen, some become engineers, some become writers, but we all want one thing very much—to become men like our teacher.

---

scold：責罵

閱讀上面的短文，選擇正確答案。

(　) 1. The writer always thought that _____.
   A. a wise and good person would never become rich
   B. a wise and good person would become rich
   C. a wise teacher would become rich
   D. a good teacher would never become rich at all

(　) 2. The writer's teacher is the following except that _____.
   A. he is very kind　　　　　　B. he never scolds his students
   C. he works very hard　　　　D. he likes to help his students

(　) 3. What's the meaning of the underlined sentence "***He is kinder to us than anyone whom I've ever known***"?
   A. He is the kindest person I know.
   B. He is kinder than many people I know.

C. I know many people who are kinder than he.

D. Only a few people are kinder than he.

(　　) 4. From this passage, we know that the writer _____.

A. is now working 　　　　　　　B. is now still a student

C. is now a doctor 　　　　　　　D. is now also a teacher

(　　) 5. Which is NOT true according to this passage?

A. The writer is proud of his teacher very much.

B. The writer may become a teacher in the future, too.

C. It's very easy to be a wise and good teacher.

D. The teacher may become rich if he gets down to business.

【參考譯文】

　　我過去一直認爲，一個聰明而善良的人應該能發家致富，但今年我意識到這種想法並非一貫正確。

　　我是從老師身上明白這一點的。他既聰明又善良，但並不富裕，因爲他的工作是教師，所以他的收入並不高。如果他放棄教學轉而經商，或許他能掙到更多的錢。但他很爲自己的教師身份而自豪，以致把幫助別人當作快樂之源。

　　他從早到晚待在學校努力工作。當我們向他求教時，他總是面帶微笑。他對我們的善意超過了我認識的任何人。我覺得學歷史或數學肯定比學做他這樣一個人要容易得多。當我們做錯事時，他會批評我們，但這種批評是爲了讓我們做得更好。

　　我們都希望能一直跟他學下去，但這是不可能的。我們中的有些人可能會成爲醫生、商人、工程師、作家，但我們都懷有一個迫切的希望——希望成爲像他一樣的人。

---

income n. 　收入，所得：They always live within their income. 他們總是量入為出。

take pleasure in 喜歡做（某事），以...為樂：He seems to take a great pleasure in doing such things. 他看來非常喜歡幹這類事。/I take pleasures in introducing the next speaker. 我非常高興介紹下一位發言人。

scold v. 　責備，訓斥：Don't scold the child. It's not his fault. 不要責備孩子，這不是他的過失。

【參考答案】

1. B 　　　　2. B 　　　　3. A 　　　　4. B 　　　　5. C

Unit 77

題材　人間溫情　　詞數　236　　建議閱讀時間　4.5分鐘

It was very cold outside my car. I did not want to get out of it __1__ we passed by a cafe. Suddenly I noticed a short old man, __2__ with some bits of cloth, shaking with the cold. He was waiting for anyone who would __3__ him a coin or a cup of hot coffee.

I asked my husband to go over and hand this old man something. He __4__ into my husband's face, smiled and said, "Thank you." I felt so happy and I wished the old man could live __5__ the cold night.

I was sure to meet him again and find out how he was the next day, as I have to pass this way every day. I did so the next evening, and he remembered the __6__ and came up to my window and __7__ at me. This time I offered him a bag of food. He reached out for the bag and I gave him my hand. He __8__ the food, smiled and said, "May God bless you." I looked at the old man and he __9__ me think of my father.

I do hope all of us will remember that maybe one day, it could happen to one of us, so please do not pass by a __10__ person without offering at least a word of love and a kind smile or an act of kindness of any kind.

---
give sb. one's hand 伸手與某人握手：She gave him her hand frankly, and wished him a good journey. 她真誠地伸出手來與他握手，並祝他一路平安。(注意：give sb. a hand 意為「說明某人」。)

閱讀上面的短文，選擇正確答案。

(　) 1. 　A. after 　　　　B. when 　　　　C. before 　　　　D. if

(　) 2. 　A. covered 　　B. tied 　　　　C. filled 　　　　D. provided

(　) 3. 　A. send 　　　B. leave 　　　C. greet 　　　　D. accept

(　) 4. 　A. watched 　　B. knocked 　　C. came 　　　　D. looked

(　) 5. 　A. in 　　　　B. through 　　C. under 　　　　D. off

(　) 6. 　A. office 　　　B. gift 　　　　C. car 　　　　D. shop

(　) 7. 　A. smiled 　　B. pointed 　　C. called 　　　D. shouted

(　) 8. 　A. held 　　　B. ordered 　　C. dropped 　　D. received

(　) 9. 　A. got 　　　　B. forced 　　C. made 　　　　D. allowed

(　　) 10.　A. quiet　　　　B. sick　　　　C. poor　　　　D. shy

◖參考譯文◗

　　車外很冷。當我們路過一家咖啡館時，我不想下車。突然，我注意到一個矮個子老人，他衣衫襤褸，凍得發抖。他正在等人給他一枚硬幣或一杯熱咖啡。

　　我讓丈夫過去給老人一點東西。他看著我丈夫的臉，微笑著說：「謝謝。」我感到很高興，希望老人能熬過這個寒冷的夜晚。

　　我確信第二天能見到他，並能看到那時他怎樣了，因為我每天都要從這條路經過。第二天晚上我的確又見到了他，而他還記得這輛車，於是跑到車窗前沖我微笑。這次我給了他一袋食品。他伸手接過袋子，我和他握了握手。他拿著食品，笑著說："願上帝保佑你。"我看著老人，他讓我想起了自己的父親。

　　我確實希望所有人都能記住：也許有一天，這樣的事可能發生在我們中的任何一個人身上。所以，大家在經過一個窮人身旁時，請至少說一句暖心的話並給予友善的微笑或做出任何一種善意的舉動。

◖參考答案◗

| 1. B | 2. A | 3. B | 4. D | 5. B |
| 6. C | 7. A | 8. A | 9. C | 10. C |

Unit 78

題材 人物　　　　詞數 191　　　　建議閱讀時間 4 分鐘

When Ben Franklin was only a boy, he always wanted to know about things. He was always asking his father and brothers "What?" and "How?" and "Why?"

They couldn't always tell him what he wanted to know. When they couldn't tell him, Ben tried to find out the answers by himself.

Many times Ben did find out things that no one knew before. The other boys would say, "That Ben Franklin! He's always finding out something new!"

Ben lived close to the water. He liked to go there to see the boats. He saw how the wind blew them across the water.

One day Ben said to himself, "Why can't the wind help me float across the water? And I'm going to try." Ben got his big kite. He took hold of the kite's string and ran with it. The wind took the kite up into the air. Then Ben jumped into the water.

The wind blew the kite high into the air. Ben began to float across the water. Soon he was on the other side.

One boy shouted, "Look at Ben floating across the water! His kite takes him to the other side without any work!"

"Yes," said another. "He's always finding new ways to do things."

---
float：飄、浮　string：繩子

閱讀上面的短文，選擇正確答案。

(　　) 1.　When he was only a child, Ben _____.
　　　　A. liked to fly a kite by himself
　　　　B. always asked easy questions
　　　　C. always liked to play with water
　　　　D. always liked to find out how things worked

（　　）2.　His father and brothers _____.
　　　　A. couldn't answer all his questions
　　　　B. could answer all his questions
　　　　C. tried hard to find out something new for him
　　　　D. were too busy to answer his questions

（　　）3.　How did Ben Franklin float across the water?
　　　　A. The other boy took him across it.
　　　　B. The water carried him across it.
　　　　C. The flying kite took him across it.
　　　　D. A boat took him across it.

（　　）4.　He found out many things that _____.
　　　　A. children didn't know　　　　B. his father and brothers knew
　　　　C. people didn't know　　　　D. most people knew

【參考譯文】

　　當班·富蘭克林還是個孩子時，他已經有了求知的欲望。他總是問父親和兄長「什麼」、「怎樣」以及「為什麼」之類的問題。

　　但他們無法總是回答出他提出的所有問題。當他們解答不了時，班就試著自己尋找答案。

　　有很多次，班的確發現了一些從無人知曉的事物。其他男孩會說，「那就是班·富蘭克林。他一直在探索新鮮事物。」

　　班住的地方靠近水邊。他喜歡去水邊看船。他明白了風是怎樣吹動船駛過水面的。

　　一天，本自言自語道：「為什麼不能讓風幫我渡河？我想試試。」班找來一隻大風箏。他抓住風箏線跟著風箏跑起來。風把風箏吹上了天空。班連蹦帶跳地踩進水裏。

　　風吹著風箏越飛越高。班開始從水面上漂過。很快，他就到了對岸。

　　一個男孩叫道：「看，班漂過水面了。他的風箏毫不費力就把他帶到了對岸！」

　　「是的，」另一個男孩說，「他總能找到做事的新方法。」

---

blow v.　（blew，blown）　吹，吹動：The wind blew my papers away. 風吹走了我的文件。/I tried to blow the dust off the desk. 我想吹掉桌子上的灰。

float v.　飄浮，浮動：Oil floats on water. 油浮在水面上。

string n.　繩，線，帶：I cut a length of string to tie up the package. 我剪下一段細繩來捆紮包裹。

【參考答案】

　　1. D　　　　　2. A　　　　　3. C　　　　　4. C

Unit 79

| 題材 | 異國文化 | 詞數 | 185 | 建議閱讀時間 | 3.5 分鐘 |

People in different countries have different ways of doing things. Something that is __1__ in one country may be quite impolite in another.

In Britain, you mustn't lift you bowl to your __2__ when you are having some liquid food. But it's __3__ in China. And in Japan you even needn't worry about making __4__ while you are having it. It shows that you are enjoying it. But people in Britain think it is bad manners. If you are a visitor in Mongolia, what manners do they wish __5__ to have? They wish you to give a loud "burp" __6__ you finish eating. Burping shows that you like the food.

In Britain, you should try not to __7__ your hands on the table when you're having a meal. In Mexico, however, guests are expected to keep their hands on the table during a meal. But in Arab countries you must be very careful with your hands. You __8__ eat with your left hand. Arabs consider it very __9__ manners eating with left hands. So when you are in other countries, __10__ carefully and follow them.

---
impolite：不禮貌的　burp：打嗝

閱讀上面的短文，選擇正確答案。

(　) 1.　A. bad 　　　B. useful 　　　C. terrible 　　　D. polite

(　) 2.　A. mouth 　　B. nose 　　　C. ears 　　　D. eyes

(　) 3.　A. same 　　B. different 　　C. important 　　D. difficult

(　) 4.　A. faces 　　B. noises 　　　C. mistakes 　　D. friends

(　) 5.　A. them 　　B. her 　　　C. you 　　　D. him

(　) 6.　A. after 　　B. before 　　　C. if 　　　D. until

(　) 7.　A. give 　　B. take 　　　C. bring 　　　D. put

(　) 8.　A. needn't 　B. mustn't 　　C. shouldn't 　D. may not

(　) 9.　A. different 　B. important 　C. good 　　　D. bad

(　) 10.　A. see 　　B. look 　　　C. read 　　　D. watch

◀參考譯文▶

　　不同國家的人們做事的方式也不同。在某國被認為是禮貌的行為到了另一國就可能變得很不禮貌。

　　在英國，當你吃流食時，你不能把碗端到嘴邊。但在中國就不同。而在日本，你甚至不必擔心弄出響聲，因為這表明你很愛吃。但英國人會認為這是粗魯的行為。假如你訪問蒙古國，他們希望你以什麼樣的方式吃飯呢？他們希望你吃完後打一個大大的「飽嗝」。打飽嗝意味著你喜歡吃這樣東西。

　　在英國，吃飯時儘量不要把手放在桌上。然而在墨西哥，主人卻希望客人們把手放到桌上。在阿拉伯國家，你要非常小心自己的手。你千萬不能用左手吃東西。阿拉伯人認為這是非常粗魯的。因此，當你來到別的國家，要小心觀察別人的吃法，然後照樣子做。

> **impolite**　adj. 不禮貌的，粗魯的：It was very impolite not to write and thank them. 不寫信向他們致謝是很不禮貌的。
> **burp**　n. 飽嗝兒 ‖ v. 打嗝

◀參考答案▶

1. D	2. A	3. B	4. B	5. C
6. A	7. D	8. B	9. D	10. D

Unit 80

題材 奇聞軼事　　**詞數** 181　　**建議閱讀時間** 4 分鐘

It doesn't matter when or how much a person sleeps, but everyone needs some rest to stay alive. That's what all doctors thought, until they heard about AI Herpin. AI Herpin, it was said, never slept. Could this be true? The doctors decided to see this strange man themselves.

AI Herpin was 90 years old when the doctors came to his home in New Jersey. They thought for sure that he got some sleep of some kind. So they stayed with him and watched every movement he made. But they were surprised. Though they watched him hour after hour and day after day, they never saw Herpin sleeping. In fact, he did not even own a bed. He never needed one.

The only rest that Herpin sometimes got was sitting in a comfortable chair and reading newspapers. The doctors were puzzled by this strange continuous sleeplessness. They asked him many questions, hoping to find an answer. They found only one answer that might explain his condition. Herpin remembered some talk about his mother having been injured several days before he was born. But that was all. Was this the real reason? No one could be sure.

Herpin died at the age of 94.

---

continuous：持續的　condition：狀況　injured：受傷的

閱讀上面的短文，選擇正確答案。

(　) 1. The main idea of this passage is that _____.
　　　A. large numbers of people do not need sleep
　　　B. a person was found who actually didn't need any sleep
　　　C. everyone needs some sleep to stay alive
　　　D. people can live longer by trying not to sleep

(　) 2. The doctors came to visit Herpin, expecting _____.
　　　A. to cure him of his sleeplessness
　　　B. to find that his sleeplessness was not really true
　　　C. to find out why some old people didn't need any sleep
　　　D. to find a way to free people from the need of sleeping

（　　）3.　After watching him closely, the doctors came to believe that AI Herpin
_____.

A. needed some kind of sleep　　B. was too old to need any sleep

C. needed no sleep at all　　D. often slept in a chair

（　　）4.　One reason that might explain Herpin's sleeplessness was _____.

A. his mother's injury before he was born

B. that he had gradually got rid of the sleeping habit

C. his magnificent physical condition

D. that he hadn't got a bed

（　　）5.　AI Herpin's condition could be regarded as _____.

A. a common one　　B. one that could be cured

C. a bad one　　D. a rare one

【參考譯文】

　　一個人什麼時候睡、睡多長時間都沒有關係，但他一定要有睡眠才能活著。所有的醫生都這麼認為，直到有一天他們聽說了阿爾·赫爾平的故事。據說，阿爾·赫爾平從不睡覺。這會是真的嗎？醫生決定親自去看看這個奇人。

　　當醫生們來到位於新澤西的阿爾·赫爾平的家中時，他已經 90 歲了。醫生認為，他肯定需要某種睡眠。因此，無論他幹什麼，他們都和他待在一起注意觀察。但他們很吃驚。儘管他們日復一日一刻不停地看著他，他們從未看到赫爾平睡覺。實際上，他甚至沒有床。因為他從不需要。

　　赫爾平休息的唯一方式是有時候坐在舒服的椅子上讀報紙。醫生對這種奇怪的連續不眠現象感到困惑。他們問了他許多問題，希望能找到答案。他們只發現，有一個答案或許能解釋這種現象。赫爾平記得有人說過，他母親在生他前幾天曾受過傷。但也只有這些。這是真正的原因嗎？沒有人能肯定。

　　赫爾平于 94 歲時去世。

movement　n.　運動，活動，移動：She mounted the horse in an easy movement. 她動作自如地上了馬。

own　v.　擁有：They dreamed of owning their own house. 他們夢想著有自己的房子。

puzzled　adj.　困惑的：You look very puzzled about something. 你好像對什麼事情很困惑。

sleepless　adj.　失眠的，不眠的：Late in the night，sleepless and troubled, he got up and went for a walk. 深夜，他憂心忡忡，難以入眠，索性起床散步。‖ **sleeplessness**　n. 不眠的現象

【參考答案】

1. B　　2. B　　3. C　　4. A　　5. D

筆記欄

筆記欄

筆記欄

筆記欄

筆記欄

筆記欄

筆記欄

筆記欄

筆記欄